Python

The Ultimate Beginner's Guide!

Andrew Johansen

Table of Contents

Introduction

I want to thank you and congratulate you for purchasing this book...

"Python: The Ultimate Beginner's Guide!"

This book contains proven steps and strategies on learning Python Programming quickly and easily.

Python is a powerful and flexible programming language. It uses concise and easy-to-learn syntax which enables programmers to write more codes and develop more complex programs in a much shorter time.

Python: The Ultimate Beginner's Guide provides all essential programming concepts and information you need to start developing your own Python program. The book provides a comprehensive walk-through of Python programming in a clear, straightforward manner that beginners will appreciate. Important concepts are introduced through a step-by-step discussion and reinforced by relevant examples and illustrations. You can use this book as a guide to help you explore, harness, and gain appreciation of the capabilities and features of Python.

Thanks again for purchasing this book, I hope you enjoy it!

Chapter 1   Getting Acquainted with Python

Python is an open source, high-level programming language developed by Guido van Rossum in the late 1980s and presently administered by Python Software Foundation. It came from the ABC language that he helped create early on in his career.

Python is a powerful language that you can use to create games, write GUIs, and develop web applications.

It is a high-level language. Reading and writing codes in Python is much like reading and writing regular English statements. Because they are not written in machine-readable language, Python programs need to be processed before machines can run them.

Python is an interpreted language. This means that every time a program is run, its interpreter runs through the code and translates it into machine-readable byte code.

Python is an object-oriented language that allows users to manage and control data structures or objects to create and run programs. Everything in Python is, in fact, first class. All objects, data types, functions, methods, and classes take equal position in Python.

Programming languages are created to satisfy the needs of programmers and users for an effective tool to develop applications that impact lives, lifestyles, economy, and society. They help make lives better by increasing productivity, enhancing communication, and improving efficiency. Languages die and become obsolete when they fail to live up to expectations and are replaced and superseded by languages that are more powerful. Python is a programming language that has stood the test of time and has remained relevant across industries and businesses and among programmers, and individual users. It is a living, thriving, and highly useful language that is highly recommended as a first programming language for those who want to dive into and experience programming.

Advantages of Using Python

Here are reasons why you would prefer to learn and use Python over other high level languages:

Readability

Python programs use clear, simple, and concise instructions that are easy to read even by those who have no substantial programming background. Programs written in Python are, therefore, easier to maintain, debug, or enhance.

Higher productivity

Codes used in Python are considerably shorter, simpler, and less verbose than other high-level programming languages such as Java and C++. In addition, it has well-designed built-in features and standard library as well as access to third party modules and source libraries. These features make programming in Python more efficient.

Less learning time

Python is relatively easy to learn. Many find Python a good first language for learning programming because it uses simple syntax and shorter codes.

Runs across different platforms

Python works on Windows, Linux/UNIX, Mac OS X, other operating systems and small-form devices. It also runs on microcontrollers used in appliances, toys, remote controls, embedded devices, and other similar devices.

Chapter 2   Installing Python

Installing Python in Windows

To install Python, you must first download the installation package of your preferred version from this link:

https://www.python.org/downloads/

On this page, you will be asked to choose between the two latest versions for Python 2 and 3: Python 3.5.1 and Python 2.7.11. Alternatively, if you are looking for a specific release, you can scroll down the page to find download links for earlier versions.

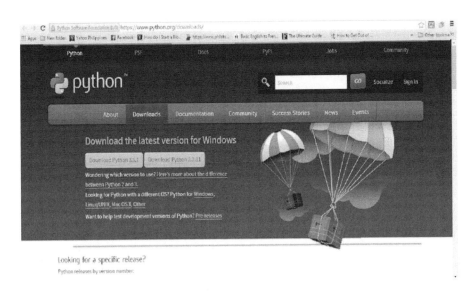

You would normally opt to download the latest version, which is Python 3.5.1. This was released on December 7, 2015. However, you may opt for the latest version of Python 2, 2.7.11. Your preferences will usually depend on which version will be most usable for your project. While Python 3 is the present and future of the language, issues such as third party utility or compatibility may require you to download Python 2.

Installing Python in Mac

If you're using a Mac, you can download the installation package from this link:

https://www.python.org/downloads/mac-osx/

Running the Installation file:

Once you're finished with the download, you can proceed to installation by clicking on the downloaded .exe file. Standard installation will include IDLE, pip, and documentation.

Chapter 3   Interacting with Python

Python is a flexible and dynamic language that you can use in different ways. You can use it interactively when you simply want to test a code or a statement on a line-by-line basis or when you're exploring its features. You can use it in script mode when you want to interpret an entire file of statements or application program.

To use Python interactively, you can use either the Command Line window or the IDLE Development Environment.

Command Line Interaction

The command line is the most straightforward way to work with Python. You can easily visualize how Python works as it responds to every completed command entered on the >>> prompt. It may not be the most preferred interaction with Python, but it is the simplest way to explore how Python works.

Starting Python

There are different ways to access Python's command line depending on the operating system installed on your machine:

•   If you're using Windows, you can start the Python command line by clicking on its icon or menu item on the Start menu.

•   You may also go to the folder containing the shortcut or the installed files and click on the Python command line.

- If you're using GNU/Linux, UNIX, and Mac OS systems, you have to run the Terminal Tool and enter the Python command to start your session.

We use commands to tell the computer what to do. When you want Python to do something for you, you have to instruct it by entering commands that it is familiar with. Python will then translate these commands to instructions that your computer or device can understand and execute.

To see how Python works, you can use the print command to print the universal program "Hello, World!"

1.   Open Python's command line.

2.   At the >>>prompt, type the following:

    print("Hello, World!")

3.   Press enter to tell Python that you're done with your command. Very quickly, the command line window will display Hello, World! on the following line:

Python responded correctly because you gave it a command in a format that it requires. To see how it responds when you ask it to print the same string using a wrong syntax for the print command, type and enter the following command on the Python command prompt:

Print("Hello, World!")

This is how Python will respond:

Syntax error: invalid syntax

You'll get syntax error messages whenever you enter invalid or incomplete statements. In this case, you typed print with a capital letter which is a big no to a case-sensitive language like Python.

If you're just using Python interactively, you can do away with the print command entirely by just typing your statement within quotes such as "Hello, World!"

Exiting Python

To exit from Python, you can type any of these commands:

quit()
exit()
Control-Z then press enter

IDLE: Python's Integrated Development Environment (IDE)

The IDLE (Integrated Development and Learning Environment) tool is included in Python's installation package but you can choose to download more sophisticated third party IDEs.

The IDLE tool offers a more efficient platform to write your code and work interactively with Python. You can access IDLE on the same folder where you found the command line icon or on the start menu. As soon as you click on the IDLE icon, it will take you to the Python Shell window.

The Python Shell Window

The Python Shell Window has dropdown menus and a >>>prompt that you have seen earlier in the command line window. Here you can type and enter statements or expressions for evaluation in the same way that you used the command line earlier. This time however, IDLE's editing menu allows you to scroll back to your previous commands, cut, copy, and paste previous statements and make modifications. IDLE is quite a leap from the command line interaction.

The Python Shell window has the following menu items: File, Edit, Shell, Debug, Options, Windows, and Help.

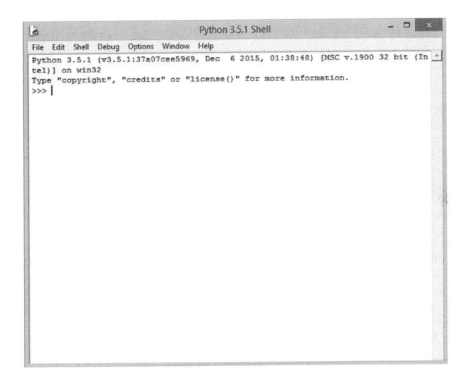

The Shell and Debug menus provide capabilities you would find useful when creating larger programs.

The Shell menu allows you to restart the shell or search the shell's log to find the most recent reset.

The Debug Menu has useful menu items for tracing the source file of an exception and highlighting the erring line. The Debugger option will usher in an interactive debugger window that will allow you to step through the running program. The Stack Viewer option displays the current Python stack through a new window.

The Options window allows you to configure IDLE to suit your Python working preferences.

The Help option opens Python Help and documentation.

The File Window

The items on the File menu allows you to create a new file, open an old file, open a module, and/or save your session. When you click on the 'New File' option, you will be taken to a new window, a simple and standard text editor where you can type or edit your code. Initially, this file window is named 'untitled' but its name will soon change as you save your code.

The File window's menu bar varies only slightly with the Shell Window. It doesn't have the 'Shell' and 'Debug' menu found in the Shell Window but it introduces two new menus: the Run and the Format menu. When you choose to Run your code on the file window, you can see the output on the Shell Window.

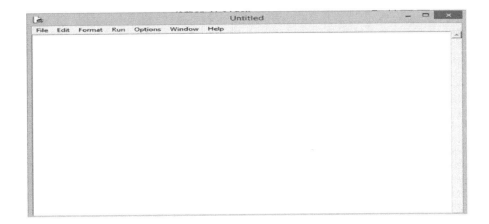

The Script Mode

When working in script mode, you won't automatically see results the way you would in interactive mood. To see an output from a script, you'll have to run the script and/or invoke the print() function within your code.

Chapter 4   Python Syntax

Python syntax refers to the set of rules that defines how human users and the system should write and interpret a Python program. If you want to write and run your program in Python, you must familiarize yourself with its syntax.

Keywords

Python keywords are reserved words in Python that should not be used as variable, constant, function name, or identifier in your code. Take note of these keywords if you don't want to run into errors when you execute your program:

and	assert
break	class
continue	def
del	elif
else	except
exec	finally
for	from
global	if
import	in
is	lambda
not	or
pass	print
raise	return
try	while
with	yield

Python Identifiers

A Python Identifier is a name given to a function, class, variable, module, or other objects that you'll be using in your Python program. Any entity you'll be using in Python should be appropriately named or identified as they will form part of your program.

Here are Python naming conventions that you should be aware of:

- An identifier can be a combination of uppercase letters, lowercase letters, underscores, and digits (0-9). Hence, the following are valid identifiers: myClass, my_variable, var_1, and print_hello_world.

- Special characters such as %, @, and $ are not allowed within identifiers.
- An identifier should not begin with a number. Hence, 2variable is not valid, but variable2 is acceptable.

- Python is a case-sensitive language and this behavior extends to identifiers. Thus, Labor and labor are two distinct identifiers in Python.

- You cannot use Python keywords as identifiers.

- Class identifiers begin with an uppercase letter, but the rest of the identifiers begin in lowercase.

- You can use underscores to separate multiple words in your identifier.

You should always choose identifiers that will make sense to you even after a long gap. Hence, while it is easy to set your variable to c = 2, you might find it more helpful for future reference if you use a longer but more relevant variable name such as count = 2.

Using Quotations

Python allows the use of quotation marks to indicate string literals. You can use single, double, or triple quotes but you must start and end the string with the same type. You would use the triple quotes when your string runs across several lines.

Python Statements

Statements are instructions that a Python interpreter can execute. When you assign a value to a variable, say my_variable = "dog", you're making an assignment statement. An assignment statement may also be as short as c = 3. There are other kinds of statements in Python, like *if* statements, *while* statements, *for* statements, etc.

Multi-line statements

A statement may span over several lines. To break a long statement over multiple lines, you can wrap the expression inside parentheses, braces, and brackets. This is the preferred style for handling multi-line expressions. Another way to wrap multiple lines is by using a backslash (\) at the end of every line to indicate line continuation.

Indentation

While most programming languages such as Java, C, and C++ use braces to denote blocks of code, Python programs are structured through indentation. In Python, blocks of codes are defined by indentation not as a matter of style or preference but as a rigid language requirement. This principle makes Python codes more readable and understandable.

A block of code can be easily identified when you look at a Python program as they start on the same distance to the right. If it has to be more deeply nestled, you can simply indent another block further to the right. For example, here is a segment of a program defining car_rental_cost:

```
def car_rental_cost(days):
        cost = 35 * days
        if days >= 8:
                cost -= 70
        elif days >= 3:
                cost -= 20
        return cost
```

You have to make sure that the indent space is consistent within a block. When you use IDLE and other IDEs to input your codes, Python intuitively provides indentation on the subsequent line when you enter a statement that requires indentation. Indentation, by convention, is equivalent to 4 spaces to the right.

Comments

When writing a program, you'll find it helpful to put some notes within your code to describe what it does. A comment is very handy when you have to review or revisit your program. It will also help another programmer who might need to go over the source code. You can write comments within your program by starting the line with a hash (#) symbol. A hash symbol tells the Python interpreter to ignore the comment when running your code.

For multi-line comments, you can use a hash symbol at the beginning of each line. Alternatively, you can also wrap multi-line comment with triple quotes.

Chapter 5   Variables and Data Types

Variables

A variable is like a container that stores values that you can access or change. It is a way of pointing to a memory location used by a program. You can use variables to instruct the computer to save or retrieve data to and from this memory location.

Python differs significantly from languages such as Java, C, or C++ when it comes to dealing with variables. Other languages declare and bind a variable to a specific data type. This means that it can only store a unique data type. Hence, if a variable is of integer type, you can only save integers in that variable when running your program.

Python is a lot more flexible when it comes to handling variables. If you need a variable, you'll just think of a name and declare it by assigning a value. If you need to, you can change the value and data type that the variable stores during program execution.

To illustrate these features:

In Python, you declare a variable by giving it a value:

my_variable = 10

Take note that when you are declaring a variable, you are not stating that the variable my_variable is equal to 10. What the statement actually means is "my_variable is set to 10".

To increase the value of the variable, you can enter this statement on the command line:

```
>>>my_variable = my_variable + 3
```

To see how Python responded to your statement, invoke the print command with this statement:

```
>>>print(my_variable)
```

You'll see this result on the next line:

13

To use my_variable to store a literal string "yellow", you'll simply set the variable to "yellow":

```
>>>my_variable = "yellow"
```

To see what's currently store in my_variable, use the print command:

```
>>>print(my_variable)
```

On the next line, you'll see:

yellow

Data Types

Python handles several data types to facilitate the needs of programmers and application developers for workable data. These include strings, numbers, Booleans, lists, date, and time.

Strings

A string is a sequence of Unicode characters that may be a combination of letters, numbers, and special symbols. To define a string in Python, you can enclose the string in matching single or double quotes:

>>>string1 = "I am enclosed in single quotes."
>>>string2 = "I am enclosed in double quotes."

If a literal string enclosed in single quotes contains a single quote, you'll have to place a backslash (\) before the single quote within the string to escape the character. For example:

>>> string3 = 'It doesn\'t look good at all.'

To print string3:

>>> print(string3)
It doesn't look good at all.

Of course, you wouldn't have to do this if you used double quotes to enclose the string:

>>>string3 = "It doesn't seem nice"

Similarly, you'll have to place a backslash before a double quote if your string is enclosed in double quotes:

>>>txt = "He said: \"You should get the same results no matter how you choose to enclose a string.\""

>>> print(txt)
He said: "You should get the same results no matter how you choose to enclose a string."

21

Strings may be indexed or subscripted. In Python, indexing starts from 0 (zero) instead of 1. Hence, a string's first character has a zero index.

To illustrate how string indexing works in Python, define the string "Hello Python" on the command line:

>>>s = "Hello Python"

This is how Python would index the string:

-12	-11	-10	-9	-8	-6	-6	-5	-4	-3	-2	-1
H	e	l	l	o		P	y	t	h	o	n
0	1	2	3	4	5	6	7	8	9	10	11

To access the first character on the string you just created, type and enter the variable name s and the index 0 within square brackets like this:

>>>s[0]

You'll get this output:
'H'

Accessing the first character is easy because you know that its index number is zero. You do not have this advantage when you want to access the last character on the string.

To access the last character, you can use this expression:

>>>s[len(s)-1]

You'll get the output:

'n'

22

The expression introduces you to the *len* function. There is actually an easier way to access the last item on the string:

```
>>>s[-1]
'n'
```

To access the penultimate character:

```
>>>s[-2]
'o'
```

Besides indexing, you can use other functions and mathematical operators on a string.

Concatenating Strings

Strings can be added together with plus (+) operator. To concatenate the string "Hello Python":

```
>>> "Hello" + "Python"
'HelloPython'
```

Repeating Strings

You can easily repeat strings or its concatenation with the * operator. For example:

Entering "**^**" * 5 will yield:

```
'**^****^****^****^****^**'
```

You'll get the same result with this:

```
>>>s = "**^**"
>>>s * 5
'**^****^****^****^****^**'
```

23

Getting the Size of Strings

You can get the size of a string with the len() function. For example, to get the size of the string "World":

```
>>>len("World")
5
```

Slicing Strings

You can create substrings with the slicing notation. You can do this by placing two indices (separated by a colon) within square brackets. The first index marks the start of the substring while the second index indicates the index number of the first character you don't want to include in the substring.

For example:

```
>>>"Program"[3:5]
```

will result in:
```
'gr'
```

```
>>>"Program"[3:6]
```

will yield:

```
'gra'
```

Another way of doing this is by storing "Program" to a variable and manipulating the variable to produce the desired result:

```
>>>p = "Program"
>>>p [3:6]
'gra'
```

If you want the substring to start from a character to the end of the original string, you can just omit the second index. For example:

```
>>>p = "Program"
>>>p [4:]
'ram'
```

Conversely, if you want your substring to start from the first character of the original string, you can omit the first index and write the last index to be included on the substring. For example:

```
>>>p = "Program"
>>>p [:4]
'Prog'
```

The lower() and upper() function

If you have a string like "Grand River" and you have decided that you need your data to be all in lower case, you can use the lower() function to print the string in lower case.

Example:

```
>>>c = "Grand River"
>>>print (c.lower())
grand river
```

Supposing you need you string to be all capitalized, you can invoke the *upper()* function to print the string in uppercase.

Example:

```
>>>print (c.upper())
```

The str() method

The *str()* function makes strings out of non-strings character. This allows programmers to print non-string characters as if they are string characters. This is very handy when you want, for instance, to print an integer along with strings.

Example:

```
>>>pi =3.1416
>>>str(pi)
'3.1416'

>>>print("This my favorite number: " + str(pi))
This my favorite number: 3.1416
```

Numbers

Numeric Data Types

One of the many conveniences of using Python is that you don't really have to declare a numeric value to distinguish its type. Python can readily tell one data type from another when you write and run your statement. It has four built-in numeric data types. Python 3 supports three types: integer, floating-point numbers, and complex numbers. Long integers ('long') no longer form a separate group of integers but are included in the 'int' or integer category.

1. *Integer (int)*

Integers are whole numbers without decimal point. They can be positive or negative as long as they don't contain a decimal point that would make a number a floating number, a distinct numeric type. Integers have unlimited size in Python 3.

The following numbers and literals are recognized by Python:

Regular integers

Examples: 793, -254, 4

Octal literals (base 8)

To indicate an octal number, you will use the prefix 0o or 0O (zero followed by either a lowercase or uppercase letter 'o').

Example:

```
>>>a = 0O7
>>>print(a)
7
```

Hexadecimal literals (base 16)

To indicate hexadecimal literals, you will use the prefix '0X' or '0x" (zero and uppercase or lowercase letter 'x').

Example:

```
>>>hex_lit = 0xA0C
>>>print(hex_lit)
2572
```

Binary literals (base 2)

To signify binary literals, you'll use the prefix '0B' or '0b' (zero and uppercase or lowercase 'b').

Example:

```
>>> c = 0b1100
>>> print(c)
12
```

Converting Integers to their String Representation

Earlier, you have seen how the print command converted literals to their equivalent in integers. Python makes it possible for you to work the other way around by converting integers to their literal representation. To convert an integer into its string representation, you can use the functions *hex()*, *bin()*, and *oct()*.

Examples:

To convert the integer 7 to its octal literal, type and enter oct(7) on the command prompt. You'll get the output '007':

```
>>>oct(7)
'007'
```

Here is what happens when you convert the integer 2572 to a hexadecimal literal:

```
>>>hex(2572)
'0xa0c'
```

Finally, see what happens when you use the bin() function to convert the integer 12 to its binary string:

```
>>>bin(12)
'0b1100'
```

You can store the result to a variable by defining a variable with the hex(), bin(), and oct() functions:

For example:

```
>>>x = hex(2572)
>>>x
'0xa0c'
```

To see the object type created and stored in the variable x, you can use and enter the command type():

```
>>>type(x)
```

You should get this result:

```
<class 'str'>
```

2. Floating-point numbers

Also known as floats, floating-point numbers signify real numbers. Floats are written with a decimal point that segregates the integer from the fractional numbers. They may also be written in scientific notation where the uppercase or lowercase letter 'e' signifies the 10th power:

```
>>>6.2e3
6200.0
```

```
>>>6.2e2
620
```

3. *Complex numbers*

Complex numbers are pairs of real and imaginary numbers. They take the form 'a + bJ' where 'a' is a float and the real part of the complex number. On the other side is bJ where 'b' is a float and J or its lowercase indicates the square root of an imaginary number, -1. This makes 'b' the imaginary part of the complex number.

Here are examples of complex numbers at work:

```
>>>a = 2 + 5j
>>>b = 4 − 2j
>>>c = a + b
>>>print(c)
(6 + 3j)
```

Complex numbers are not extensively used in Python programming.

Conversion of Number Type

You can expect Python to convert expressions with mixed types of numbers to a common type to facilitate evaluation. In some situations, however, you may have to convert one number type to another explicitly, like when the conversion is required by a function parameter. You can type the following expressions to convert a number to another type:

To convert x to a float: >>>float(x)

Example:

```
>>>float(12)
12.0
```

To convert x to a plain integer: int(x)

```
>>>int(12)
12
```

To convert x to a complex number: type complex(x)

```
>>>complex(12)
(12+0j)
```

Date and Time

Most applications require date and time information to make it work efficiently and effectively. In Python, you can use the function datetime.now() to retrieve the current date and time. The command datetime.now() calls on a built-in Python code which gives the current date and time.

To get the date and time from Python, encode the following on the command prompt:

```
>>> from datetime import datetime
>>> datetime.now()
datetime.datetime(2016, 3, 10, 2, 16, 19, 962429)
```

The date and time in this format is almost unintelligible and you might want to get a result that is more readable. One way to do this is by using 'strftime' from Python's standard library.

Try entering these commands and see if you'll get the format you like.

```
>>>from time import strftime
>>> strftime("%Y-%m-%d %H:%M:%S")
'2016-03-10 02:20:03'
```

Boolean Data Type

Comparisons in Python can only generate one of two possible responses: True or False. These data types are called booleans.

To illustrate, you can create several variables to store Boolean values and print the result:

```
bool_1 = 4 == 2*3
bool_2 = 10 < 2 * 2**3
bool_3 = 8 > 2 * 4 + 1
print(bool_1)
print(bool_2)
print(bool_3)
```

The Python Shell will display these results:

```
False
True
False
```

Lists

A list is a data type that can be used to store any type and number of variables and information.

You can define and assign items to a list with the expression:

```
my_list = [item_1, item_2, item_3]
```

Python also allows creation of an empty list:

```
my_list = []
```

To illustrate, let's create a list of colors:

colors = ["red", "orange", "yellow", "green", "indigo", "white"]

Since this is an indexed list, the first item on colors has zero as its index.

To access the first item on the list, you can print the color with the command:
>>> print(colors[0])
red

To print the color name of the third color on the list, you can enter:

>>> print(colors[4])
indigo

To see how many colors are on the list, you can use the len() function:

>>> len(colors)
6

There are only six colors on your list but you want to have all seven colors of the rainbow in your list. To see what colors are on the list, you can use the print to see what color might be missing:

>>> print(colors)
['red', 'orange', 'yellow', 'green', 'indigo', 'white']

It appears that the colors list doesn't just lack one color name. It also has one member that should not have been included – 'white'. To remove 'white' from the list, you can use the remove() method:

>>> colors.remove("white")

You can view the updated list with the print command:

>>> print(colors)
['red', 'orange', 'yellow', 'green', 'indigo']

The list is still short of 2 colors – violet and blue.

To add violet to your colors list, you can use the append command:

>>> colors.append("violet")

Let's check out the updated list with the print command:

>>> print(colors)
['red', 'orange', 'yellow', 'green', 'indigo', 'violet']

The color 'violet' was added to the end of the list. Now, you only need to add one more color - blue. Let's say you want to have 'blue' inserted between 'green' and 'indigo'.

You can use Python's insert()method with the syntax:
list.insert(index, obj)

The parameters are index and object. Index refers to the position where you want the new item to be located. The object is the item you want to insert.

Applying the syntax to the above example, you'll have the command:

>>> colors.insert(4, "blue")

To see the new list:

>>> print(colors)

['red', 'orange', 'yellow', 'green', 'blue', 'indigo', 'violet']

Slicing lists

You can also slice lists in the same way that you slice strings.

For example, if you only want to display the colors 'green', 'blue', and 'indigo', with index of 3, 4, 5 respectively, you can use this command:

>>> colors[3:6]
['green', 'blue', 'indigo']

Dictionary

A dictionary is like a list but instead of looking up an index to access values, you'll be using a unique key, which can be a number, string, or tuple. Dictionary values can be anything but the keys must be an immutable data type. A colon separates a key from its value and all are enclosed in curly braces. Here is the dictionary structure:

d = {key_1 : a, key_2 : 2, key_3 : ab}

An empty dictionary will have this format:

d = {}

A dictionary can be a very useful tool for storing and manipulating key-value pairs such as those used in phone books, directory, menu, or log-in data. You can add, modify, or delete existing entries within the dictionary.

To see how dictionaries actually work, you can create a dictionary named menu with dish and prices pairs:

35

menu = {"spam" : 12.50, "carbonara" : 20, "salad" : 15 }
To see how many key-value pairs are stored in the dictionary, you can use the len() function:

```
>>>len(menu)
3
```

To print the current entries in the menu dictionary:

```
>>> print(menu)
{'salad': 15, 'carbonara': 20, 'spam': 12.5}
```

To add another entry in the menu dictionary, you can use this format:

d[key_4 : b]

Applying this structure to the menu dictionary, you can add the dish-price entry of cake : 6 with:

```
menu["cake"] = 6
```

To see the updated menu, use the print command:

```
>>> print(menu)
{'spam': 12.5, 'cake': 6, 'carbonara': 20, 'salad': 15}
```

Assuming you no longer want to include spam in your menu, you can easily do so with the del command:

```
>>> del menu["spam"]
```

To see the modified list after deleting spam:

{'cake': 6, 'carbonara': 20, 'salad': 15}

You might want to change the values in any of the keys at one point. For instance, you need to change the price of carbonara from 20 to 22. To do that, you'll just assign a new value to the key with this command:

>>> menu["carbonara"] = 22

You can use the print command once more to see the updated menu:

>>> print(menu)
{'cake': 6, 'carbonara': 22, 'salad': 15}

If you want to remove all entries in the dictionary, you can use the function

dict.clear()

To clear all entries in the menu:

>>>dict.clear(menu)

Use the print command to see what happened to the menu dictionary:

>>> print(menu)
{}

The Python Shell displayed an empty dictionary with the clear command. Now that it contains no data at all, you might decide to delete the dictionary. You can do so with the del command:

del dict

To delete the menu dictionary:

del menu

To see what happened, use the print command.

```
>>> print(menu)
Traceback (most recent call last):
  File "<pyshell#19>", line 1, in <module>
    print(menu)
NameError: name 'menu' is not defined
```

You got an error message because menu no longer exists.

Chapter 6   Python Basic Operators

Python operators allow programmers to manipulate data or operands. Here are the types of operators supported by Python:

- Arithmetic Operators
- Assignment Operators
- Relational or Comparison Operators
- Logical Operators
- Identity Operators
- Bitwise Operators
- Membership Operators

Arithmetic Operators

Python does a good job of processing mathematical expressions with its basic arithmetic operators. You can easily make programs to automate tasks such as computing tax, tips, discounts, or rent.

+	Addition	adds the value of the left and right operands
-	Subtraction	subtracts the value of the right operand from the value of the left operand
*	Multiplication	multiplies the value of the left and right operand
/	Division	divides the value of the left operand by the right operand
**	Exponent	performs exponential calculation
%	Modulus	returns the remainder after dividing the left operand with the right operand
//	Floor Division	division of operands where the solution is a quotient left after removing decimal numbers

Addition, subtraction, multiplication, and division are the most basic operators and are invoked by entering the following expressions:

Addition:

>>>1 + 3
4

Subtraction:

>>>10 − 4
6

Multiplication:
>>>4 * 2
8

Division:
>>>10 / 2
5.0

Exponent

Exponential calculation is invoked by raising the first number to the power defined by the number after the ** operator:

>>>2**3   2 raised to the power of 3
8

Modulus

The modulus operator gives the remainder after performing division:

>>>17 % 5

Floor Division

Floor division, on the other hand, returns the quotient after removing fractional numbers:

>>>17 // 5
3

Using Basic Operators to Compute Sales Tax, Tip, and Total Bill

To put your knowledge of variables, data types, and operators to good use, you can design a simple program that will compute the sales tax and tip on a restaurant meal.

Meal cost	$65.50
Sales tax rate	6.6%
Tip	20% of meal + tax

First, set up a variable meal to store the food cost:

meal = 65.50

Next, set up the tax and tip variable. Assign both variables the decimal value of the percentages given. You can do this by using 100 as divisor.

tax = 6.6 / 100
tip = 20 / 100

Your tip is based on meal cost and the added sales tax so you need to get the total amount of the meal and the sales tax. One way to do this is by simply creating a new variable to store the total cost of the meal and tax. Another way is by reassigning the variable meal so that it stores both values:

meal = meal + meal * tax

Now that you have reassigned meal to take care of the meal cost and tax, you're ready to compute for the tip. This time, you can set a new variable to store the value of the tip, meal, and tax. You can use the variable total to hold all values:

total = meal * tip

Here's your code to compute for the total bill amount:

```
meal = 65.50
tax = 6.6 / 100
tip = 20 / 100
meal = meal + meal * tax
total = meal + meal * tip
```

If you're using the file editor in IDLE, you can save the file in a filename of your choice and Python automatically appends the .py extension. As you may have noticed, the file editor will always prompt you to save your file before it does anything about your code. Just like when naming other data files and types, you should use a filename that's descriptive of the file. In this case, a filename like BillCalculator should do the trick.

To get the total amount, go to the Python Shell and type total:
```
>>>total
83.78760000000001
```

Now you have the bill amount: 83.78760000000001

If you're using the line command window, you can simply enter the above code on a per line basis.

This simple program shows how straightforward Python programming is and how useful it could be in automating tasks. Next time you eat out, you can reuse the program by simply changing the figures on your bill calculator. Think forward and visualize how convenient it could be if you could put your code in a bigger program that will simply ask you to input the bill amount instead of accessing the original code. You can do that with Python.

Assignment Operators

These operators are useful when assigning values to variables:

Operators	Function
=	assigns the value of the right operand to the left operand
+= add and	adds the value of the right and left operand and assigns the total to the left operand
-= subtract and	deducts the value of the right operand from the value of the left operand and assigns the new value to the left operand
*= multiply and	multiplies the left and right operand and assigns the product to the left operand
/= divide and	divides the left operand with the value of the right operand and assigns the quotient to the left operand
**= exponent	performs exponential operation on the left operand and assigns the result to the left operand
//= floor division and	performs floor division on the left operand and assigns the result to the left operand

43

= Operator

You have seen this operator at work in previous chapters when you have assigned different values to variables. Examples:

a = c
a = b + c
a = 8
a = 8 + 6
s = "I love Python."

+= add and

The 'add and' (+=) operator is simply another way to express x = x + a so that you'll end up with the statement x += a.

-= subtract and

The 'subtract and' (-=) operator is equivalent to the expression x = x − a and is expressed with the statement x-=a

*= multiply and

The 'multiply and' (*=) operator is the equivalent of the statement x = x * a and is expressed with x*=a.

/= divide and

The 'divide and' (/=) operator is like saying x = x/a and is expressed with the statement x/=a.

%= modulus and

The 'modulus and' (%=) operator is another way to say x = x % a where you'll end up instead with the expression x%=a.

//= floor division and

The 'floor division and' is equivalent to the expression x = x//a and takes the form x//=a.

Relational or Comparison Operators

Relational operators evaluate values on the left and right side of the operator and return the relation as either True or False.

Here are the relational operators in Python:

Operator	Meaning
==	is equal to
<	is less than
>	is greater than
<=	is less than or equal to
>=	is greater than or equal to
!=	is not equal to

Examples:

```
>>> 8 == 6+2
True

>>> 6 != 6
False

>>> -1 > 0
False

>>> 7 >= 5
True
```

Logical Operators

Python supports 3 logical operators:

or
and
not

x or y   If the first argument, x, is false, then it evaluates the second argument, y. Else, it evaluates x.

x and y   If x is false, then it evaluates x. Else, if x is   true, it evaluates y.

not x   If x is false, then it returns True. If x is true, it returns False.

Examples:

```
>>> (8>9) and (2<9)
False

>>> (2>1) and (2>9)
False

>>> (2==2) or (9<20)
True

>>> (3!=3) or (9>20)
False


>>> not (8 > 2)
False

>>> not (2 > 10)
```

True

Precedence of Python Operators

Python operators are evaluated according to a set order or priority:

	Description	Operators
1	Exponentiation	**
2	Ccomplement, unary plus, and minus	~, +, -
3	Multiplication, division, modulo, and floor division	*, /, %, //
4	addition and subtraction	+ -
5	Right and left bitwise shift	>>, <<
6	Bitwise 'AND'	&
7	Regular `OR' and Bitwise exclusive 'OR'	|, ^
8	Comparison operators	<= < > >=
9	Equality operators	== !=
10	Assignment operators	=, +=, -=, *-, /=, %= //= **=
11	Identity operators	is, is not
12	Membership operators	in, not in
13	Logical operators	or, and, not

Chapter 7   Python's Built-in Functions

Functions provide efficiency and structure to a programming language. Python has many useful built-in functions to make programming easier, faster, and more powerful.

The input() Function

Programs usually require input that can come from different sources: keyboard, mouse clicks, database, another computer's storage, or the internet. Since the keyboard is the most common way to gather input, Python provided its users the input() function. This function has an optional parameter called the prompt string.

Once the input function is called, the prompt string will be displayed on the screen and the program flow stops until the user has entered an input. The input is then interpreted and the input() function returns the user's input as a string.

To illustrate, here is a sample program that collects keyboard input for name and age:

```
name = input("May I know your name? ")
print("It's a pleasure to meet you " + name + "!")
age = input("Your age, please? ")
print("So, you're " + age + " years old, " + name + "!")
```

Before you save the code, take a close look at the string to be printed on the second line. You'll notice that there is a blank space after 'you' and before the double quote. This space ensures that there will be a space between 'you' and the 'name' input when the print command is executed. The same convention can be seen on the 4th line with the print command where 'you're' is separated by a single space from the 'age' input and 'old' is separated by a space from the 'name' input.

Save the code as info_input.py and run it.

```
info_input.py                                          ×
File  Edit  Format  Run  Options  Window  Help
name = input ("May I know your name? ")
print ("It's a pleasure to meet you " + name + "!")
age = input ("Your age, please? ")
print ("So, you're " + age + " years old, " + name + "!")
```

The Python Shell will display the string on the first line:

May I know your name?

A response is needed at this point and the program stops executing until a keyword input is obtained. Let's type and enter the name Jeff to see what happens:

It's a pleasure to meet you Jeff!
Your age, please?

The program has now proceeded to the next input function and is waiting for the keyboard input. Let's enter 22 as Jeff's age and see what the program does next:

So, you're 22 years old, Jeff!

49

The program printed the last string on the program after a keyboard response was obtained. Here is the entire output on the Python Shell:

May I know your name? Jeff
It's a pleasure to meet you Jeff!
Your age, please? 22
So, you're 22 years old, Jeff!

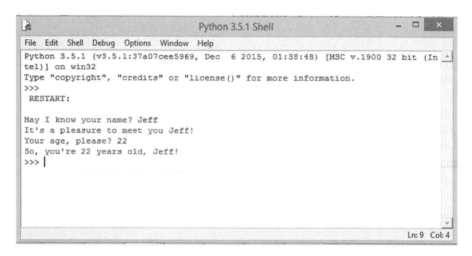

The range() function

Python has a more efficient way to handle a series of numbers and arithmetic progressions and this is by using one its built-in functions: range(). The range function is particularly useful in 'for loops'.

Here is an example of the *range()* function:

```
>>> range(5)
range(0, 5)
```

The expression range(5) above generates an iterator that progresses integers from zero and ends with 4 (5-1). To show the list of numbers, you can use the command list(range(n)):

>>>list(range(5))
[0, 1, 2, 3, 4]

You can exercise more control over the list output by calling the range() function with two arguments:

range (begin, end)

Example:

>>> range(5, 9)
range(5, 9)

To show the list:

>>> list (range(5, 9))
[5, 6, 7, 8]

The above examples of *range()* demonstrated an increment of 1. You can change the way Python increments the number by introducing a third argument, the 'step'. It can be a negative or positive number, but never zero.

Here is the format:

range(begin, end, step)

Example:

>>> range(10, 71, 5)
range(10, 71, 5)

Invoking list, we'll see this sequence of numbers:

>>> list (range(10, 71, 5))
[10, 15, 20, 25, 30, 35, 40, 45, 50, 55, 60, 65, 70]

The print() Function

Python 3 turned *print* from a statement into a function. Hence, you must always enclose your print parameters within the round parentheses.

Examples:

```
print("This is Python 3 print function)
print(s)
print(5)
```

The *print()* function can print any number of values within the parentheses; they must be separated by commas. For example:

```
a = 3.14
b = "age"
c = 32

print("a = ", a, b, c)
```

The result:

a = 3.14 age 32

The Python shell displayed values with blank spaces between them.

abs()

The abs() function returns the absolute value of a single number. It takes an integer or float number as argument and always returns a positive value.

Examples:

```
>>> abs(-10)
10
```

```
>>> abs(5)
10
```

When complex numbers are used as argument, the abs() function returns its magnitude:

```
>>> abs(3 + 4j)
5.0
```

max()

The max() function takes two or more arguments and returns the largest one.

Examples:

```
>>> max(9, 12, 6, 15)
15
```

```
>>> max(-2, -7, -35, -4)
-2
```

min()

The min() function takes two or more arguments and returns the smallest item.

Examples:

```
>>> min(23, -109, 5, 2)
-109

>>> min(7, 26, 0, 4)
0
```

type()

The type() function returns the data type of the given argument.

Examples:

```
>>> type("This is a string")
<class 'str'>

>>> type(12)
<class 'int'>

>>> type(2 +3j)
<class 'complex'>

>>> type(215.65)
<class 'float'>
```

len()

The len() function returns the length of an object or the number of items in a list given as argument.

Examples:

```
>>> len("pneumonoultramicroscopicsilicovolcanoconiosi")
44
```

```
>>> s = ("winter", "spring", "summer", "fall")
>>> len(s)
4
```

Here is a list of Phyton's built-in functions:

abs()	all()	any()
ascii()	bin()	bool()
bytearray()	bytes()	callable()
chr()	classmethod()	compile()
complex()	delattr()	dict()
dir()	divmod()	enumerate()
eval()	exec()	filter()
float()	format()	frozenset()
getattr()	globals()	hasattr()
hash()	help()	hex()

id()	import__()	input()
int()	isinstance()	issubclass()
iter()	len()	list()
locals()	map()	max()
memoryview()	min()	next()
object()	oct()	open()
ord()	pow()	print()
property()	range()	repr()
reversed()	round()	set()
setattr()	slice()	sorted()
staticmethod()	str()	sum()
super()	tuple()	type()
vars()	zip()	

Chapter 8   Conditional Statements

Conditional statements are common among programming languages and they are used to perform actions or calculations based on whether a condition is evaluated as true or false. If-then-else statements or conditional expressions are essential features of programming languages and they make programs more useful to users.

The if-then-else statement in Python has the following basic structure:

```
if condition1:
    block1_statement
elif condition2:
    block2_statament
else:
    block3_statement
```

This structure will be evaluated as:

If condition1 is True, Python will execute block1_statement. If condition1 is False, condition2 will be executed. If condition2 is evaluated as True, block2_statement will be executed. If condition2 turns out to be False, Python will execute block3_statement.

To illustrate, here is an if-then-else statement built within the function 'your_choice':

```
def your_choice(answer):
    if answer > 5:
        print("You are overaged.")
    elif answer <= 5 and answer >1:
        print("Welcome to the Toddler's Club!")
    else:
```

```
        print("You are too young for Toddler's Club.")

print(your_choice(6))
print(your_choice(3))
print(your_choice(1))
print(your_choice(0))
```

You will get this output on the Python Shell:

```
You are overaged.
None
Welcome to the Toddler's Club!
None
You are too young for Toddler's Club.
None
You are too young for Toddler's Club.
None
```

Conditional constructs may branch out to multiple 'elif' branches but can only have one 'else' branch at the end. Using the same code block, another elif statement may be inserted to provide for privileged member of the Toddler's club: 2 year-old kids.

```
def your_choice(answer):
    if answer > 5:
        print("You are overaged.")
    elif answer <= 5 and answer >2:
        print("Welcome to the Toddler's Club!")
    elif answer == 2:
        print("Welcome! You are a star member of the Toddler's
Club!")
    else:
        print("You are too young for Toddler's Club.")

print(your_choice(6))
print(your_choice(3))
print(your_choice(1))
```

```
print(your_choice(0))
print(your_choice(2))
```

You are overaged.
None
Welcome to the Toddler's Club!
None
You are too young for Toddler's Club.
None
You are too young for Toddler's Club.
None
Welcome! You are a star member of the Toddler's Club!
None

Chapter 9   Loops

A loop is a programming construct that enables repetitive processing of a sequence of statements. Python provides two types of loops to its users: the 'for loop' and the 'while loop'. The 'for' and 'while' loops are iteration statements that allow a block of code (the body of the loop) to be repeated a number of times.

The For Loop

Python implements an iterator-based 'for loop'. It is a type of 'for loop' that iterates over a list of items through an explicit or implicit iterator.

The loop is introduced by the keyword 'for' which is followed by a random variable name which will contain the values supplied by the object.

This is the syntax of Python's 'for loop':

```
for variable in list:
        statements
else:
        statements
```

Here is an example of a 'for loop' in Python:

```
pizza = ["New York Style Pizza", "Pan Pizza", "Thin n Crispy Pizza", "Stuffed Crust Pizza"]
for choice in pizza:
    if choice == "Pan Pizza":
      print("Please pay $16. Thank you!")
    print("Delicious, cheesy " + choice)
else:
    print("Cheesy pan pizza is my all-time favorite!")
print("Finally, I'm full!")
```

Run this and you'll get the following output on Python Shell:

Delicious, cheesy New York Style Pizza
Please pay $16. Thank you!
Delicious, cheesy Pan Pizza
Delicious, cheesy Thin n Crispy Pizza
Delicious, cheesy Stuffed Crust Pizza
Cheesy pan pizza is my all-time favorite!
Finally, I'm full!

Using a break statement

A Python break statement ends the present loop and instructs the interpreter to starts executing the next statement after the loop. It can be used in both 'for' and 'while' loops. Besides leading the program to the statement after the loop, a break statement also prevents the execution of the 'else' statement.

To illustrate, a break statement may be placed right after the print function of the 'if statement':

```
pizza = ["New York Style Pizza", "Pan Pizza", "Thin n Crispy
Pizza", "Stuffed Crust Pizza"]
for choice in pizza:
    if choice == "Pan Pizza":
        print("Please pay $16. Thank you!")
        break
    print("Delicious, cheezy " + choice)
else:
    print("Cheezy pan pizza is my all-time favorite!")
print("Finally, I'm full!")
```

The Python Shell will now show:

Delicious, cheezy New York Style Pizza
Please pay $16. Thank you!

Finally, I'm full!

Using Continue Statement

The continue statement brings back program control to the start of the loop. You can use it for both 'for' and 'while' loops.

To illustrate, the continue statement may be placed right after the print function of the 'for loop' to replace the   break statement:

```
pizza = ["New York Style Pizza", "Pan Pizza", "Thin n Crispy
Pizza", "Stuffed Crust Pizza"]
for choice in pizza:
   if choice == "Pan Pizza":
      print("Please pay $16. Thank you!")
      continue
   print("Delicious, cheesy " + choice)
else:
   print("Cheesy pan pizza is my all-time favorite!")
print("Finally, I'm full!")
```

The output will be:

Delicious, cheesy New York Style Pizza
Please pay $16. Thank you!
Delicious, cheesy Thin n Crispy Pizza
Delicious, cheesy Stuffed Crust Pizza
Cheesy pan pizza is my all-time favorite!
Finally, I'm full!

Using the range() Function with the for Loop

The range() function can be combined with the 'for loop' to supply the numbers required by the loop. In the   following example, the range(1, x+1) provided the numbers 1 to 50 needed by the 'for loop' to add the sum of 1 until 50:

```
x = 50

total = 0
for number in range(1, x+1):
    total = total + number

print("Sum of 1 until %d: %d" % (x, total))
```

The Python Shell will display:

```
l.py
Sum of 1 until 50: 1275
```

The While Loop

A Python 'while loop' repeatedly carries out a target statement while the condition is true. The loop iterates as long as the defined condition is true. When it ceases to be true and becomes false, control passes to the first line after the loop.

The 'while loop' has the following syntax:

```
while condition
    statement

statement
```

Here is a simple 'while loop':

```
counter = 0
while (counter < 10):
    print('The count is:' , counter)
    counter = counter + 1
```

```python
print("Done!")
```

If you run the code, you should see this output:

```
l.py
The count is: 0
The count is: 1
The count is: 2
The count is: 3
The count is: 4
The count is: 5
The count is: 6
The count is: 7
The count is: 8
The count is: 9
Done!
```

Using Pass Statement

The pass statement tells the Python interpreter to 'do nothing'. The interpreter simply continues with the program's execution whenever the pass statement is encountered. This attribute makes it a good placeholder whenever Python syntactically requires a line but the program itself does not require action. It can be very useful when you're creating a program and you need to focus on specific areas of your code, but you still want to reserve some loops or test run the incomplete code.

Here is how you would use a pass statement to fill gaps within a code:

```python
def function_name(x):
    pass
```

Chapter 10   User-Defined Functions

A function is a set of statements that perform a specific task, a common structuring element that allows you to use a piece of code repeatedly in different parts of a program. The use of functions improve a program's clarity and comprehensibility and makes programming more efficient by reducing code duplication and breaking down complex tasks into more manageable pieces. Functions are also known as routines, subroutines, methods, procedures, orsubprograms.

They can be passed as arguments, assigned to variables, or stored in collections.

A user-defined Python function is created or defined by the def statement and follows the syntax:

def function_name(parameter list):
        function body/statements

The indented statements make up the body of the function and are executed when the function is called. Once the function is called, parameters inside round brackets become arguments.

Function bodies can have more than one return statement which may be placed anywhere within the function block. Return statements end the function call and return the value of the expression after the return keyword. A return statement with no expression returns the special value 'None'. In the absence of a return statement within the function body, the end of the function is indicated by the return of the value 'None'.

The docstring is an optional statement after the function title which explains what the function does. While it is not mandatory, documenting your code with a docstring is a good programming practice.

Here is a simple function that prints I love Pizza!

```
def love_pizza():
    print "I love Pizza!"
```

Here is a function with a parameter and return keyword:

```
def absolute_value(number):

    if number >= 0:
        return number
    else:
        return -number

print(absolute_value(3))
print(absolute_value(-5))
```

In the above example, number is the parameter of the function absolute_value. It acts as a variable name and holds the value of a passed in argument.

Here is the output when the above code is run:

```
3
5
```

Following is a function with an if-then-else statement.

```
def shutdown(yn):
    if yn.lower() == "y":
        return("Closing files and shutting down")
    elif yn.lower() == ("n"):
        return("Shutdown cancelled")
    else:
```

```
    return("Please check your response.")

print(shutdown("y"))
print(shutdown("n"))
print(shutdown("x"))
```

Python Shell will display:

```
Closing files and shutting down
Shutdown cancelled
Please check your response.
```

Function can take more than one parameter and use them for computations:

```
def calculator(x, y):
    return x * y + 2

print(calculator(2,6))
print(calculator(3,7))
```

Run the code and you'll get the output:
```
14
23
```

Functions can call other functions

Functions can perform different types of actions such as do simple calculations and print text. They can also call another function.

For example:

```
def members_total(n):
```

```
    return n * 3

def org_total(m):
    return members_total(m) + 5
```

To see what you code does, enter the following print commands:

```
print(org_total(2))
print(org_total(5))
print(org_total(10))
```

You'll get these results:
11
20
35

Scope and lifetime of a local variable

A variable's scope refers to a program's sections where it is recognized. Variables and parameters defined within a function have a local scope and are not visible from outside of the function. On the other hand, a variable's lifetime refers to its period of existence in the memory. Its lifetime coincides with the execution of a function which ends when you return from the function. A variable's value is discarded once the return is reached and a function won't be able to recall a variable's value from its previous value.

Chapter 11 Classes and Object-Oriented Programming

Python is an object-oriented programming language, which means that it manipulates and works with data structures called objects. Objects can be anything that could be named in Python – integers, functions, floats, strings, classes, methods, etc. These objects have equal status in Python. They can be used anywhere an object is required. You can assign them to variables, lists, or dictionaries. They can also be passed as arguments. Every Python object is a class. A class is simply a way of organizing, managing, and creating objects with the same attributes and methods.

In Python, you can define your own classes, inherit from your own defined classes or built-in classes, and instantiate the defined classes.

Class Syntax

To define a class, you can use 'class', a reserved keyword, followed by the classname and a colon. By convention, all classes start in uppercase. Forexample:

```
class Students:
    pass
```

To create a class that takes an object:

```
class Students(object)
```

The init () method

69

Immediately after creating an instance of the class, you have to call the   init   () function. This function initializes the objects it creates. It takes at least the argument 'self', a Python convention, which gives identity to the object being created.

Examples:

class Students:
    def__init__(self) :

class Employees(object):
    def__init__(self, name, rate, hours) :

A function used in a class is called a method. Hence,   the __init () function is a method when it is used to   initialize classes.

Instance Variables

When you add more arguments to the def_init_() besides the self, you'll need to add instance variables so that any instance object of the class will be associated with the instance you create.

For example:

class Employees(object):
    def__init__(self, name, rate, hours) :
        name.self = name
        rate.self = rate
        hours.self =hours

In the above example, name.self, rate.self, and hours.self are the instance variables.

When you create instances of the class Employees, each member will have access to the variables which were initialized   through the   __init__   method. To illustrate, you can create or 'instantiate' new members of the class Employees:

staff = Employees("Wayne", 20, 8)
supervisor = Employees("Dwight", 35, 8)
manager = Employees("Melinda", 100, 8)

You can then use the print command to see how the instance variables interacted with the members of the class Employees:

print(staff.name, staff.rate, staff.hours)
print(supervisor.name, supervisor.rate, supervisor.hours)
print(manager.name, manager.rate, manager.hours)

The Python Shell will display this output:

Wayne 20 8
Dwight 35 8
Melinda 100 8

Here is how the entire code was written on the editor/file window:

```
                       employees.py
File  Edit  Format  Run  Options  Window  Help
class Employees(object):
    def __init__(self, name, rate, hours):
        self.name = name
        self.rate = rate
        self.hours = hours

staff = Employees("Wayne", 20, 8)
supervisor = Employees("Dwight", 35, 8)
manager = Employees("Melinda", 100, 8)

print(staff.name, staff.rate, staff.hours)
print(supervisor.name, supervisor.rate, supervisor.hours)
print(manager.name, manager.rate, manager.hours)
```

File window: employees.py

Here's the output:

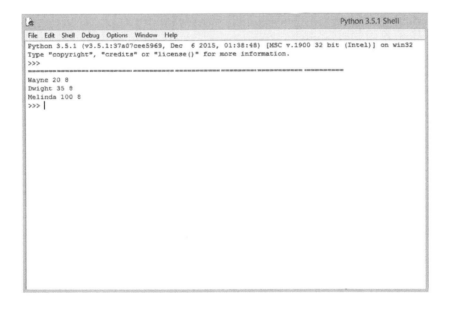

Inheritance

Inheritance is a Python process that allows one class to take on the methods and attributes of another. This feature allows users to create more complicated classes that inherit methods or variables from their parent or base classes and makes programming more efficient.

This is the syntax for defining a class that inherits all variables and function from a parent class:

class ChildClass(ParentClass):

To illustrate, you can create a new class, Resigned, that will inherit from the Employees class and take an additional variable, status:

```
class Employees(object):
    def___init___(self, name, rate, hours):
        self.name = name
        self.rate = rate
        self.hours = hours

staff = Employees("Wayne", 20, 8)
supervisor = Employees("Dwight", 35, 8)
manager = Employees("Melinda", 100, 8)

print(staff.name, staff.rate, staff.hours)
print(supervisor.name, supervisor.rate, supervisor.hours)
print(manager.name, manager.rate, manager.hours)

class Resigned(Employees):
    def___init___(self, name, rate, hours, status):
        self.name = name
        self.rate = rate
        self.hours = hours
        self.status = status
```

exemp_1 = Resigned("Dorothy", 32, 8, "retired")
exemp_2 = Resigned("Malcolm", 48, 8, "resigned")

print(exemp_1.name, exemp_1.rate, exemp_1.hours, exemp_1.status)
print(exemp_2.name, exemp_2.rate, exemp_2.hours, exemp_2.status)

```
                              resigned.py
File  Edit  Format  Run  Options  Window  Help
class Employees(object):
    def __init__(self, name, rate, hours):
        self.name = name
        self.rate = rate
        self.hours = hours

staff = Employees("Wayne", 20, 8)
supervisor = Employees("Dwight", 35, 8)
manager = Employees("Melinda", 100, 8)

print(staff.name, staff.rate, staff.hours)
print(supervisor.name, supervisor.rate, supervisor.hours)
print(manager.name, manager.rate, manager.hours)

class Resigned(Employees):
    def __init__(self, name, rate, hours, status):
        self.name = name
        self.rate = rate
        self.hours = hours
        self.status = status

exemp_1 = Resigned("Dorothy", 32, 8, "retired")
exemp_2 = Resigned("Malcolm", 48, 8, "resigned")

print(exemp_1.name, exemp_1.rate, exemp_1.hours, exemp_1.status)
print(exemp_2.name, exemp_2.rate, exemp_2.hours, exemp_2.status)
```

Here is the output on the Python Shell when the code is executed;

```
Python 3.5.1 Shell                                                                      _ □ x
File  Edit  Shell  Debug  Options  Window  Help
Python 3.5.1 (v3.5.1:37a07cee5969, Dec  6 2015, 01:38:48) [MSC v.1900 32 bit (Intel)] on win32
Type "copyright", "credits" or "license()" for more information.
>>>
 RESTART: C:/Users/Shawn Michaels/AppData/Local/Programs/Python/Python35-32/resigned.py
Wayne 20 8
Dwight 35 8
Melinda 100 8
Dorothy 32 8 retired
Malcolm 48 8 resigned
>>> |
```

Chapter 12   Templates

In this chapter, we'll be looking at templating--what it is, how to use it, and the reason why it should be used. So what is a Template? Well, the template is just like it sounds: the formatted layout that you fill in with important things. The Python template module is part of the string module, as it uses a string to define the template. The template's key feature is that it allows data to change without having to edit the application every time.

How It Works

So how do templates work? Well, the template class takes a string of the template. Within the string, you use placeholder variable names with a preceding dollar sign to depict that it's a placeholder. You can then substitute values into the template with the substitute method using a dictionary, where the keys of the dictionary match the placeholder variable names.

The return string is the template with all the values, rather than the placeholders. It should also be noted that a placeholder variable name should follow the same naming conventions as Python.

So let's go ahead and make something to explain this. We will make a simple output program that will output information about the user's item cart. We'll use a template to format the output and fill it in with the user's cart's information. So let's go ahead and create a Python cart named 'cart.py.' We recommend you use *Vim* as your Python text editor since it provides the best usability out of all the text editors out there.

Go ahead and create the 'cart.py' Python file using Vim by typing the syntax below in your terminal:

    $ vim cart.py

First, we're going to need the template module. To invoke the template module. Type the syntax below in the first line of your Python code:

from string import Template

Next, we're going to create the cart with all the items inside using Python code. To do this, type the code below:

```
def Main ():
    cart = []
    cart.append(dict(item="Coke", price=8, qty=2))
    cart.append(dict(item="Cake", price=12, qty=1))
    cart.append(dict(item="Fish", price=32, qty=4))
```

The code above is out main function. The portion of the code that's highlighted in red is the cart list. This list holds all the information about the cart. Now this information could come from a database, from a file, or from anything of the sort. However, for the sake of our example's simplicity, we just hard coded all the information for now.

As you can see, we integrated a dictionary function into your code, hence the keyword 'dict.' We also made use of keywords such 'item', 'price', 'qty' to hold information such as the item's name, its value, and the items quantity inside the cart.

Now that we have our cart, we now have to work on our output. For this, we'll need to create a template. Type the code below after your main function:

```
t= Template("$qty x $item = $price")
total = o
print "Cart:"
```

So basically, out template is done. Those values highlighted in red will be replaced by the values in our cart. As you also may have noticed, we created another variable named 'total.' It is the variable that will keep the total of all the prices of the items in the cart. The 'total' variable is then followed by a 'print' function, which instructs the Python compiler to display the total of 'cart.'

Your overall code should look just like the one below:

```python
from string import Template

def Main ():

    cart = []
    cart.append(dict(item="Coke", price=8, qty=2))
    cart.append(dict(item="Cake", price=12, qty=1))
    cart.append(dict(item="Fish", price=32, qty=4))
t= Template("$qty x $item = $price")
total = 0
print "Cart:"
```

So for the data in our cart, you need to type the code below:

```python
for data in cart:
        print t.substitute(data)
        total += data["price"]
    print "Total: " + str(total)
```

As you can see from our code, we're going substitute the data values into our template and print it out using the *print t.substitute (data)* syntax. And then, we'll get the total by adding all of the 'price' keyword in our cart list using the *total +=* *data["price"]* syntax. After getting our total, we print it using the *print "Total: " + str(total)* syntax.

To finalize our code, type in the syntax below:

78

```
if__name__ == "__main__":
        Main()
```

Your completed code should now look like the one below:

```
from string import Template

def Main ():
        cart = []
        cart.append(dict(item="Coke", price=8, qty=2))
        cart.append(dict(item="Cake", price=12, qty=1))
        cart.append(dict(item="Fish", price=32, qty=4))
        t= Template("$qty x $item = $price")
        total = 0
        print "Cart:"
        for data in cart:
                print t.substitute(data)
                total += data["price"]
        print "Total: " + str(total)
if__name__ == "__main__":
        Main()
```

After making sure that everything is typed correctly, save the cart.py file.
After saving the 'cart.py' file, run it by typing the syntax below:

```
$ Python cart.py
```

Once you type that in, you'll see the output below:

```
Cart:
2 x Coke = 8
1 x Cake = 12
4 x Fish = 32
```

Total: 52

Errors are possible in templates, but mostly they occur while you're programming them. So for debugging purposes, here are a few common ones:

No Placeholder match - This will give a KeyError. This is usually because there was no key and there's no value in the dictionary to match the placeholder.

Bad Placeholder - This one gives a ValueError. This usually occurs when the placeholder starts with an invalid character, or it doesn't exist at all.

Safe_Substitute()

We can have the template handle these problems by using the *safe substitute()* method of the template class. This will return a string no matter what. However, any unresolved keys and braces will be in the resulting string. Take a look at the example below:

Template("$name had $money"), output: "Jim had $money"

As you can see in the example above, instead of having the proper output where the keywords *name* and *money* are assigned values, only the name is assigned with one. Normally, "$money" wouldn't have been returned at all. However, with the *safe_substitute()* method, it will return a string value regardless. In this case, "$money" is that string.

Custom Delimiters

It is also possible for you to create a custom delimiter by using the subclass to override the default in the template class. This is great when the user is creating the template from the command line. So let's go ahead and edit our previous example code to use the hash symbol rather than the dollar sign.

To override the template class, first we need to create a subclass, which we'll call "MyTemplate." This subclass will take a template as a base class. Then we'll override the delimiter variables. Your code should now look like the one below:

```
from string import Template

class MyTemplate(Template):

        delimiter = '#'

def Main ():

        cart = []
        cart.append(dict(item="Coke", price=8, qty=2))
        cart.append(dict(item="Cake", price=12, qty=1))
        cart.append(dict(item="Fish", price=32, qty=4))
        t= Template("$qty x $item = $price")
        total = 0
        print "Cart:"
        for data in cart:
                print t.substitute(data)
                total += data["price"]
        print "Total: " + str(total)
if__name__== "__main__":
        Main()
```

Now that we've changed the delimiter, we're going to need to change the template. The code below has these changes to the template highlighted in red:

```
t= MyTemplate("#qty x #item = #price")
total = 0
```

81

print "Cart:"

As you can see, we've changed the word "Template" to "MyTemplate," and replaced all dollar signs into hash symbols. After you've change everything, save the file and run it. It should get the same output if every works correctly.

Now that we looked at how to use a template, let's go ahead and cover why should we use one.

Why Use Templates?

The main reason why most Python programmers use templates is that it saves time and reduces the size of the code files. Also, templates make the implementation of custom templates from the command line possible. If for example you want to change the name of all the image files inside a directory, you can just type the syntax below:

File format: MyPhoto_$n$ext=MyPhoto_0.jpg, MyPhoto_1.jpg, etc.

Templates are also extremely useful for webpages, since webpages generally always adhere to a uniform template, albeit with different data.

Important Things To Know About Templates

If needed, you can escape the delimiter by using two consecutive delimiters. Take a look at the example below:

input: "You owe me $$5"

output: you owe me $5

As you can see, the first dollar sign was used as the place holder. The second dollar sign is immediately regarded by Python as a character rather than a placeholder. You can also use custom regular expressions on templates by creating a subclass that will override the ID patent variable. By default, it is set to accept underscores and alphanumeric characters.

You can also use curly braces to identify which part of the delimiter is the placeholder and which one is the variable name. In the example below, we have the template:

"The ${place}yard is far away"

In this case, the word 'yard' is appended to the result of the placeholder. So if we use the value 'ship,' the output would be:

The shipyard is far away

Note that this could be replaced with 'farm,' or a number of other places.

Chapter 13 Argparse

In this chapter, we'll be looking at argument and option parsing--what it is, how to use it, and why it should be used. So what is Argparse? Argparse is basically a standard module that comes with Python. It allows for easy and neat option argument handling for Python programs. Argparse handles generated program usage, generates the help output, and handles formatting for the console.

How It Works

Argparse works by interfacing with the Python system module; taking the command line arguments and assessing whether they're an option or an argument. If it is neither, it is ignored. Options are a *dash* and then a *letter* or *word*. Arguments usually will just be data from the user.

These options and arguments come after the program in the command line. Take a look at the example below:

```
parser = argparse.ArgumentParser()
parser.add_argument("num", help="help text",type=int)
args=parser.parse_args()
print args.num
```

In the example above, we see the three main lines that you'll usually see when using Argparse. First, we create the argument parser. Then we use the add_argument. Inside the add_argument, we specify what type of argument it is, the help for that argument, and a type if required. We then get the arguments from the parser using the parse_args method.

Positional Arguments

Positional arguments are required arguments--arguments that are needed to make sure the program runs correctly. Positional arguments do not require a *dash* since it is not an option. Similar to the example we looked at previously, no dash is specified before the argument name 'num.'

Fibonacci Program

Now that we know how the basics work, let's have a closer look as we build a quick program to test out the Argparse module. This time, we will be creating a program that outputs the *nth* Fibonacci number. And then, we'll have a required positional argument 'num' for the program to calculate to. We'll also add the help output.

First, let's create a file called 'fibn.py.' Again, just like in the previous chapter, create and open the file using the *Vim* editor. Once you have your *fibn.py* file opened thru *Vim*, type the code below:

```
import argparse
def fib(n):
        a, b = 0, 1
        for i in range(n):
                a, b = b, a+b
        return a
def Main():
        parser = argparse.ArgumentParser()
        parser.add_argument("num", help="The Fibonacci number " + \
                "you wish to calculate.", type=int)
        args = parser.parse_args()
        result = fib(args.num)
        print "The "+str(args.num)+"th fib number is "+str(result)
if __name__ == '__main__':
        Main()
```

The example code above is mainly the main program. We've used argparse to get an argument from the user and then calculate the Fibonacci number. After making sure that everything is type correctly, go ahead and save your fibn.py file. After saving the file, run it by typing the syntax below:

$ Python fibn.py

Note that if you type the above syntax you'll get the below result:

$ usage: fibn.py [-h] num

fibn.py: error: too few arguments

The reason why we got a usage error is because we didn't give it any value when we typed in '$ Python fibn.py.' As you can probably tell, the error message itself is giving us a clue as to what the proper syntax should be when running that program. Note that it says:

$ usage: fibn.py [-h] num

This means that you should either enter -h after fibn.py, or enter a positional argument 'num.' Since our program's purpose is to calculate a Fibonacci number from a number given by the user, we must enter a number after fibn.py. Let's say for example we'll enter the number '10.' Here's how the syntax should go:

$ Python fibn.py 10

Once you enter that command syntax, it'll give the output below:

$ The 10th fib number is 55

If you enter -h instead of a number, it'll show you the help text associated with the program, like the one below:

positional arguments:

    num   The Fibonacci number you wish to calculate.

optional arguments:

   -h, --help   show this help message and exit

Optional Arguments

Optional arguments are just like they sound: optional. As an example, the -h or -help option that is built into Argparse is optional. You do not have to use it every time you run the program; only when you need help. You can create as many options as you like. Argparse will happily handle them. And just like positional arguments, the help will automatically add to the help output.

```
parser.add_argument("--quiet", help="help text", action="store_true")
```

In the above example, we have a --quiet option that will give a minimalistic output to the console. Now, let's go ahead and modify our fibn.py file. It'll still take a number to output. However, we'll add an option to also save the number into a text file using the --output option.

However, you may have noticed that not many programs use --option. Instead, they just have a simple dash and one character. We'll also quickly add a shortcut option to the output argument. So, without further ado, go ahead and open your fibn.py file if you're following along, and then we'll implement the below modifications:

```python
import argparse
def fib(n):
        a, b = 0, 1
        for i in range(n):
                a, b = b, a+b
        return a
def Main():
        parser = argparse.ArgumentParser()
        parser.add_argument("num", help="The Fibonacci number " + \
                "you wish to calculate.", type=int)
        parser.add_argument("-o","--output",help="Output the " + \
                "results to a file", action="store_true")
        args = parser.parse_args()
        result = fib(args.num)
        print "The "+str(args.num)+"th fib number is "+str(result)
        if args.output:
                f = open("fibonacci.txt", "a")
                f.write(str(result) + '\n')
if __name__ == '__main__':
        Main()
```

As you can see in the modifications that are highlighted in red, we again added another argument by typing 'parser.add_argument.' This time, however, we're taking an option. Since we want a shortcut we put '-o' as an option. However, we also need to specify a long option. To do that, we entered '--option' as one of the arguments.

After creating the options, we next created a help text. We did this by immediately entering the statement 'help="Output the results to a file" after the options. Next, we specified an action. An action is basically what we want to do when the option is called. For action, we went with "store_true." This will store true into a variable called output.

Now that we've added an extra argument, we need to do something with that argument. So after we printed out the screen, we added the code below:

```
if args.output:
    f = open("fibonacci.txt", "a")
    f.write(str(result) + '\n')
```

The code above basically tells the Python compiler to create an output file by opening a text file named fibonacci. We added an "a" argument to create and open that file in appending, so that subsequent data can be added to the file. And lastly, we're telling the Python compiler to write the string of the result into the file with a "\n" argument to go down a new line.

After saving the file, run the program by typing the syntax below:

```
$ Python fibn.py -h
```

In the code above, we're telling the Python program that we want to look at the help file. After pressing ENTER on your keyboard, you should see the result below:

```
usage: fibn.py [-h] [-o] num
positional arguments:
        num            The Fibonacci number you wish to calculate.
optional arguments:
        -h, --help          show this help message and exit
        -o, --option        Output the result to a file
```

As you can see from the result above, we now have an extra optional argument, which is the -o or --output. Now let's go ahead and try it out. Type the code below in your terminal:

```
$ Python fibn.py 10 -o
```

After typing that file and pressing the ENTER, you'll get the result below:

The 10th fib number is 55

But there is more to the result than meets the eye. Keep in mind that the -o option means that we want to output the result to a file. To see the output file, first we must take a look at the files that are in our current directory. We can do this by typing the 'ls' command in our terminal.

$ ls

After typing and entering the command above, you'll have two files in your current directory: fibn.py and fibonacci.txt. As you can see, we now have the output file having the name "fibonacci.txt," which we specified in our code. Now let's see if the data inside the output file is correct. Go ahead and type the syntax below:

$ vim fibonacci.txt

By typing the code above, we're basically opening the file using Vim. Once Vim opens the file, you'll see that the data inside is the number 55--the same number as our result.

Mutually Exclusive Arguments

Mutually Exclusive Arguments are made available in Argparse with the use of the group feature. We can create mutually exclusive groups by allowing only one option to be selected, but not both or more. It displays in the usage that the options are mutually exclusive, as well as printing out an error telling the user that they can only pick one.

So let's again modify our fibn.py program. It will still take the number to output, and it will still have an option for outputting to file. However, we'll have a mutually exclusive group for either a verbose output, or a quiet output, but not both. Argparse will tell the user off for trying to use both. Let's go back to our fibn.py code and we'll add a group.

```
1      import argparse
2      def fib(n):
3              a, b = 0, 1
4              for i in range(n):
5                      a, b = b, a+b
6              return a
7      def Main():
8              parser = argparse.ArgumentParser()
9              group = parser.add_mutually_exclusive_group()
10             group.add_argument("-v","--verbose", action="store_true")
11             group.add_argument("-q","--quiet", action="store_true")
12             parser.add_argument("num", help="The Fibonacci number " + \
13                          "you wish to calculate.", type=int)
14             parser.add_argument("-o","--output",help="Output the " + \
15                          "results to a file", action="store_true")
16             args = parser.parse_args()
17             result = fib(args.num)
18             if args.verbose:
19                     print "The "+str(args.num)+"th fib number is "+str(result)
20             elif args.quiet
21                     print result
22             else;
23                     print "Fib("+str(args.num)+") = " + str(result)
24                     if args.output:
25                     f = open("fibonacci.txt", "a")
26                     f.write(str(result) + '\n')
27      if __name__ == '__main__':
28              Main()
```

As you can see with the changes that we made to our *fibn.py* file, we created our group in line 9 of our code. And within that group we added two arguments: one for the *verbose* option and one for *quiet* option--both options have both their short and long expressions declared (e.g. -v, --verbose; -q, --quiet).

Verbose is for a really obvious output. It gives all the details on how it got that result or what's happening. The previous print statement that we had in our original code is basically a verbose output, so there's no need to modify it. We just have to declare that it is a verbose output since we've added other group arguments into our code. To declare it, we added the code in line 18, which is 'if args.vebose:'

Since we have the verbose option handled, we now have to handle the alternative option, which is *quiet*. To do that, we added an 'else if,' or *elif* statement in line 20 of our code. Of course, if we make use of an *elif* statement, we have to tell the Python compiler what to do in the event that the quiet option is not specified. In line 21 of our code, we're basically telling the Python compiler to just print the result. Nothing more.

If neither of the options are specified, we also have to tell the Python compiler what to do. Lines 22 and 23 of our code simply tells Python if neither the verbose or quiet option is executed, then else print "Fib("+str(args.num)+") = " + str(result). After you make the modifications in the *fibn.py* file, save it.

Let's now go ahead and test the modifications we just made. After saving the file, go to your Python terminal and type the syntax below:

$ Python fibn.py

Typing the above code will give you the result below:

usage: fibn.py [-h] [-v | -q] [-o] num

fibn.py: error: too few arguments

Now don't be alarmed that you received an error result. This is just normal since we didn't specify any arguments when we ran 'Python fibn.py' in the terminal. Do take note that in the usage, you can now see the *-v* and *-q* options added. Now try typing and entering the command syntax below:

$ Python fibn.py 10 -vq

So with the command example above, we've entered a number and used both the verbose and quiet options. You should get the output below:

usage: fibn.py [-h] [-v | -q] [-o] num

fibn.py: error: argument -q/--quiet: not allowed with argument -v/--verbose

As you can see with the output above, the Python compiler is basically telling you that verbose and quiet cannot be used together. Why? Well, because they are mutually exclusive arguments. Now let's try entering the syntax below:

$ Python fibn.py 10 -v

With the code above, we've entered a number and asked the compiler to render the result in verbose mode by using the -v option. The result that should get with the aforementioned command is:

The 10th fibonacci number is 55

Now let's try the command again, but this time with the *quiet* option:

$ Python fibn.py 10 -q

After typing the above command, you should get the result below:

55

Now what if we don't specify any option? Let's go ahead and try it out. Enter the command below:

$ Python fibn.py 10

With the aforementioned command, you should be getting the result below:

Fib(10) = 55

And if you want to look at the help file, type the command below:

$ Pythong fibn.py -h

The command above will yield the below result:

usage: fibn.py [-h] [-v | -q] [-o] numb

positional arguments:

    num   The Fibonacci number you wish to calculate.

optional arguments:

    -h, --help   show this help message and exit

    -v, --verbose

    -q, --quiet

    -o, --output   Output the result to a file

As you can see from the result above, we now have more optional arguments.

Why Use It?

So why would you use this Python module? Well, Argparse is a fantastic way to streamline your program for professional use. It is easy and comes standard with Python. It saves you time by constructing help and usage formats for the command line output. Overall, it allows you to make more dynamic changes to your program's operation by using simple options on execution.

Here are some useful things to know about Argparse:

- Unlike Optparse, Argparse does not natively support callback functions. However, you can create your own action class that implements a function call. They are usually easier and is less time consuming.

- Argparse also supports taking arguments from lists. This is done with the *nargs* attribute on the *add.argument()* method. You can specify the number of arguments to be expected, or you can use the plus "+" symbol to specify that you don't know how many arguments there will be, but you know there will be at least one. Just keep in mind that these go into a Python list.

Chapter 14 Regular Expressions

In this chapter, we'll be looking at what regular expressions are, how to construct simple patterns, and how to use those patterns in our Python programs. So what is a regular expression? A Regular Expressions, or RegEx for short, is a pattern matching language that was formalized by American Mathematician Stephen Kleene during the 1950s.

These expressions are used to search text to find single words, or words that follow a set of rules. Today, most programming languages support regular expressions. Those that don't usually have a library that can be used to implement them.

An expression is built with a string of characters. They are built using two types of characters:

1. Metacharacters - These are characters that have a special meaning.

2. Regular characters - These are characters that have a literal meaning.

The special meaning characters are things like square brackets, and the regular characters are things like the letters A,B or C. It can be pretty simple to pick up basic regular expressions. However, some more advance expressions can be very hard to understand and construct.

How It Works

Now we won't go into too much detail on how regular expressions work, because the algorithms are going out of the scope of this book. There are a few different algorithms--around three--that are used for regular expression evaluation. However, the most common and fastest is the DFA, or Deterministic Finite Automaton.

If you like math, feel free to look behind the mathematics of this concept. If you're going for efficiency in your program, then it may be handy to know that the DFA algorithm takes $O(2^m)$ time to construct the expression, where m is the length of the pattern, but then takes $O(n)$ time to search, where n is the length of the string being searched.

Below you can see some of the basic Metacharacters that you can use in your regular expressions:

Metacharacter	Description
.	Matches with any one character (e.g. ".at" would match sat, cat, hat)
[]	Matches with any one character contained within the brackets (e.g. "[ch]at" would match hat, cat, but not sat) (you can make use of ranges as well [a-z])
[^]	Matches with any one character that is NOT within the brackets (e.g. "[^c]at" would match sat, hat, but not cat)
^	Matches with the expression if it is located at the start of the string (e.g. "^.at" would match sat, cat, hat if located at the start of the string.)
$	Works the same as ^ but at the end (e.g. ".at$" would match sat, cat, hat if located at the end of the string.)
( )	Contains sub expressions (Think BODMAS/BOMDAS)
*	Matches the preceding element zero or multiple times (e.g. "c.*" would match any word starting with c, class, cat, coat)

There are two base methods that you can use your regular expressions with in Python: Match and Search. Match will check to see if the expression matches the entire string that it is handed, while search will check to see if there's any match anywhere in a string. It is important to keep these distinctions in mind when choosing which base method to use.

RegTest Program

Now, let's go ahead and write a small program that will test if we can get regular expressions working using match and search. We'll create a pattern to avoid confusion. We'll tell Python that it is a raw string by giving it an 'r' prefix; it will have an *r'pattern'* format.

Let's go ahead and create our regtest.py file by typing the syntax below in the terminal:

```
$ vim regtest.py
```

Once you have your regtest.py file open, type the Python code below:

```
1     import re
2     def Main():
3     line = "I think I have a firm understanding of regular
expressions"
4     matchResult = re.match(r'think', line, re.M|re.I)
5     if matchResult:
6     print "Match Found: " + matchResult.group()
7     else:
8     print "No Match was found"
9     searchResult = re.search(r'think', line, re.M|re.I)
10    if searchResult:
11    print "Search Found:" + searchResult.group()
```

```
12      else:
13          print "Nothing found in search"
14      if__name__++ '__main__'
15      Main()
```

Since we're making a program for regular expressions, we need to import regular expressions to our Python program. To do that we entered 'import re' in the first line of our code. As for our main function, we created a string variable called 'line,' and then gave it a value of "I think I have a firm understanding of regular expressions."

At line 4 of our code, we're trying to get our regular expression to look for the string 'think' in the variable line, hence matchResult = re.match(r'think', line, re.M|re.I). The 're.M' and 're.I' are basically flags that we'll talk about later. Between those two flags is the '|' symbol, which stands for piping.

Line 5 is where we start our data handling. So basically what lines 5 thru 8 means is if there is a match for the string 'think' in our variable 'matchResult', then it would print the string 'Match Found" and also what the variable 'matchResult' is, which is the word/string 'think.' Otherwise, if there is no match at all, it would print "No match was found."

For our search base method in line 9, we used the same syntax of code in line 4. However, since we're using the search base method, we changed the variable from 'matchResult' to 'searchResult.' For our search result's data handling, we used the same syntax as line 5, except we used 'searchResult' instead of 'matchResult.'

Once everything is finalized, save your work and then run the file by entering the command below:

> $ Python regtest.py

After entering the aforementioned command, you will have the result below:

No match was found

Search Found: think

Now if you remember, our 'matchResult' will only match if the string 'think' is matching the whole string in the 'line' variable. This is the reason why Python yielded a 'No match was found' output for 'matchResult.' Our 'searchResult,' however, will search for the string 'think' anywhere inside the 'line' variable, which it did find since it is the second word in the expression.

Lookup Program

Now that we know how to work with regular expressions, let's now go ahead and make a more useful program that would really make use of your knowledge of regular expressions. We'll create a command-line program that will look up a word in a text file and print out the line it was in. It will basically take two arguments:

1. The word we're searching for
2. The text file to search through

Open up *Vim* and go ahead and create a file called 'lookup.py.' After creating the lookup.py file, type the code below:

```
1       import re

2       import optparse

3       def Main():

4               parser = optparse.OptionParser("usage %prog -w <word>   -f
<file>")

5               parser.add_option('-w', dest='word', type='string', help='specify a
word to search for')
```

100

```
6              parser.add_option('-f', dest='fname', type='string', help='specify a
file to search')

7              (options, args) = parser.parse_args()

8              if (options.word == None) | (options.fname == None):

9                      print parser.usage

10                     exit(0)

11             else:

12                     word = options.word

13                     fname = options.fname

14             searchFile = open(fname)

15             lineNum = 0

16             for line in searchFile.readlines():

17                     line = line.strip('\n\r')

18                     lineNum += 1

19                     searchResult = re.search(word, line, re.M|re.I)

20                     if searchResult:

21                             print str(lineNum) + ': ' + line

22     if    name == ' main ':

23             Main()
```

After typing everything in, save it and then run the 'lookup.py' file by typing the syntax below:

$ Python lookup.py -w main -f regtest.py

The command above is basically telling Python to run the 'lookup.py' file and lookup the word 'main' from the 'regtest.py' file, which is the file we created previously. So what will happen is lookup.py will find the word 'main' within that file and then print the whole line where 'main' is situated in. It should have the output below:

```
2:      def Main():

14:     if__name__++ '___main__'

15:             Main()
```

As you can see from the output, it not only specified which line the string 'main' was located in, but it also printed the whole line. Now you have a program that you can search files with.

Optional Flags

Modifier	Description
re.I	Ignore case matching
Re.M	Makes $ match ^the start of a line and the end of a line
re.S	Makes .(dot) Match any character including the new line character
re.U	Interprets Unicode
re.X	Ignores whitespaces within the pattern

You may have noticed that at the end of the match and search methods, we made use of the 're.M' and 're.I' flags. These are called Option Flags. We use flags to alter how the regular expression is run. This is useful to make regular expressions smaller and easier to use. But you may not always want to use them, especially if your expression is designed to be really strict. The flags that we used earlier-- re.I and re.M--was in *'case insensitive'* search, and it matches the string at the start and end of a line.

Search & Replace

Search and replace is also a handy feature to use sometimes. Python implements this with the sub() method, which is short for substitute. The sub() method takes a pattern, a replacement text, and the string to replace in. There's also an optional parameter to set the maximum amount of replacements to make. By default, it is set to all instances found in the matching text.

Why to Use Regular Expression?

So why do we need to make use of regular expressions? Well, the reason why you need to make use of regular expressions is because some time in your programming career, you'll have to search through text or strings. Also, there's no point in reinventing the wheel. Regular expressions run quite efficiently and are about as good as it gets at the moment for searching strings.

Most programming languages use the same standard regular language, so understanding what patterns do and how they are constructed will prove useful for reading expressions as well. Also, do keep in mind that the more characters there are in a pattern, the longer time it takes to evaluate them. So if you're planning to use the same expression more than once, it might be a good idea to compile the pattern first, and then use that object to do matching and searching functions.

Chapter 15   Multithreading

In this chapter, we'll be looking at what threads are and how you can use them in your Python program. So what is threading basically? Well, a thread can be thought of as another program running alongside your main program. The difference between being an actual separate program and a thread, is that the thread runs within the same scope as the main program. This means that they can share data much easier than two separate programs.

However, with this gain in power comes challenges. Because a piece of shared data between two separate threads may be accessed or changed at the same time, this can cause issues of which thread will use it first or write to it first.

We can use threads for different quick tasks such as running an algorithm to get a result, or to run slow processes in the background while your main program continues. This is great for saving files in the background while the interface still responds to the user's input. Most of the time, it would be unnoticeable. However, imagine if you are saving a 5 Gigabyte file. It would take a lot longer, and you don't want your program to sit there and hang for a few minutes.

You may also want to create threads to find an answer to a problem faster. A great example would be hashing a hundred passwords with md5. You could create ten threads, each hashing the passwords they are given and returning the actual hash password, meaning the whole process that usually takes 10 seconds in one thread, now takes one second because the work is split up over ten threads.

How It Works

So how does threading work? Well, since the introduction of core processors, some smart people have written the code to interact with the operating systems to allow programs to use more than one thread. On the programming level, however, the key point to remember is that threads run alongside your main program.

In your own Windows operating system, you can open the Task Manager and it will tell you how many threads a program is using.

Timer Program

The best way to learn about threads is to actually use them. So let's go ahead and make a small timer program, so you can see how threads are actually working. Each thread will output the current time, then output again after waiting for a certain amount of time. For this example, we'll name our file 'timer.py.'

    $ Vim timer.py

After creating the file, type the Python code below:

```
1    from threading import Thread
2    import time
3
4    def timer(name, delay, repeat):
5        print "Timer: " + name + "Started"
6        while repeat > 0:
7            time.sleep(delay)
8        print name + ": " + str(time.ctime(time.time()))
```

```
9              repeat -+ 1

10             print "Timer: " + name + " Completed"

11

12     def Main ():

13     t1 = Thread(target=timer, args=("Timer1", 1, 5))

14     t2 = Thread(target=timer, args=("Timer2", 2, 5))

15             t1.start()

16             t2.start()

17

18             print "Main Complete"

19

20     if__name__== '__main__':

21             Main()
```

Since we're using both thread and time in our program, obviously we have to import both the Thread and Time modules in our program. We did that in lines 1 and 2 of our code. Next we created out timer function that will pass through the threads. In line 4 of our code, we gave our timer function a name, delay, and the amount of time to repeat the timer.

Now what our function will do first is display the string 'Timer', the name that you give it, and the string 'Started.' This can be seen in line 5. The section from lines 6 through 10 is where we can see our 'while' loop. What our 'while' loop in this case basically does is, while our *repeat*--the number of times we want the timer to repeat itself--is more than zero, it will get *time.sleep(delay)* and then print the name, a colon ':' symbol, and a current time in string format.

After doing printin, it will decrease the number of *repeat* by 1. Once the number of *repeat* reaches zero, it will print the string *'Timer,'* the name of the timer, and then the string *'Completed.'* Now that we've finished our *timer* function, let's now define our *Main* function.

That part from lines 12 through 18 is where our Main function lies. We're basically using two threads in this program. In lines 13 and 14, we created our two threads--t1 and t2-- respectively. So for T1, we define that is it a Thread whose target function is 'timer.' We also define arguments for the timer function, which is Timer1 outputting only five times with a delay of one second each time.

For T2, we define that it is also a Thread whose target function is 'timer.' We also give arguments for the timer function in T2, which is Timer 2 outputting only five times with a delay or two seconds instead of one, each time.

Now since we've created out two threads, we have to tell them to start. The code in lines 15 and 16 basically does just that--telling both threads to start. Now to show that our main function is completed, we're going to ask Python to print a message saying 'Main Complete.'

Once you entered everything correctly in *Vim*, save and run the timer.py file. You should have an output similar to the one below:

Timer: Timer1 Started

Timer: Timer2 Started

Main Complete

Timer1: Tue Aug 30 17:28:17 2016

Timer1: Tue Aug 30 17:28:18 2016

Timer2: Tue Aug 30 17:28:18 2016

Timer1: Tue Aug 30 17:28:19 2016

Timer1: Tue Aug 30 17:28:20 2016

Timer2: Tue Aug 30 17:28:20 2016

Timer1: Tue Aug 30 17:28:21 2016

Timer: Timer1 Completed

Timer2: Tue Aug 30 17:28:22 2016

Timer2: Tue Aug 30 17:28:24 2016

Timer2: Tue Aug 30 17:28:26 2016

Timer: Timer2 Completed

As you can see in the output, both timers started at the same time, each thread with their own respective timers executed their function five times before displaying a 'Timer Completed' message. You can also see from the timestamps that T1 displays output on a one second delay, while T2 displays output on a two second delay.

Asynchronous Tasks

Threads are great for asynchronous tasks--tasks that can run in the background to complete tasks that may take a long time. These days, there are hundreds, if not thousands of programs that must function in real time. Therefore, you can't afford to have the program wait for a minute while you save a file or setup a network connection. This is where threads can be really great because it allows users to still interact with the program.

Custom Threads

If you're like other programmers who do not like to write the same code over and over again, don't worry. The Python threading module allows you to create your own subclasses of threads. These are useful for making task-specific threads that can be reused, or have features added to. If you need more thread type in another program, you can just reuse the one you wrote before.

AsyncWrite Program

Now let's go ahead and create a custom thread that will write a file in the background while the program continues. The custom thread will take a string to save to a file, and a file to save it to. Because this task will actually be really quick since it is a small file, we will add a delay that will just make what's going on easier to demonstrate.

We'll also use a method of the thread called *Join*. *Join* is a method that waits for the thread to finish before continuing. We'll put this in our main function. Using Vim, create a Python file named '*asyncWrite.py*.'

    $ Vim asyncWrite.py

After creating the file, type the code below:

```
1     import threading

2     import time

3

4     class AsyncWrite(threading.Thread):

5         def __init__(self, text, out):

6             threading.Thread.__init__(self)

7             self.text = text
```

```
8                        self.out = out

9

10          def run(self):

11                       f = open(self.out, "a")

12                       f.write(self.text + '\n')

13                       f.close()

14                       time.sleep(2)

15                       print "Finished Background file write to " +
self.out

16

17      def Main():

18                  message = raw_input("Enter a string to store:")

19                  background = AsyncWrite(message, 'out.txt')

20                  background.start()

21                  print "The program can continue to run while it
writes in another thread"

22                  print 100+400

23

24                  background.join()

25                  print "Waited until thread was complete"

26

27      if__name == '__main__':

28          Main()
```

As you can see from line 1 of our code, we imported the whole threading module instead of just importing a particular subclass of the module. We also imported the time module, since we will be implementing a time delay in this program. That section of code from lines 4 through 8 is where our custom class resides.

In line 4, we created a class called AsyncWrite that has *threading.Thread* as a super class. In line 5, we defined our initializer that's going to take self, the text to save, and the out file to save it to. In line 6, what we're basically doing is have the super class *threading.Thread* initialize itself--the super class--to create a thread. Next, we set *self.text*--the text to save--equal to '*text*,' which is the text that we pass in. We also set *self.out* equal to the '*out*' that we pass in.

On line 10, we defined another function called the '*run*' function. This function takes '*self*' and nothing else. And inside this 'run' function, we're going to ask Python to open a file. As you can see in line 11 of our code, we designated the variable 'f' to open the file *self.out* in append mode, which is identified by the "a" argument. Append means that we can add lines of data to it as we go along.

On line 12, we're asking Python to write whatever data that is found on the *self.text* file, plus a next line character, on the 'f' file. Remember that 'f' is basically the opened *self.out* file that we defined on line 11. After that, we close the file in line 13 of our code. We then implement a two second time delay on the function with *time.sleep(2)*, so that we can see what's actually going on.

After a two second delay, we print the string "Finished Background file write to "+ self.out. So that's basically it. We have completed our custom class. Now, it is time to create our Main function.

Our Main function starts from line 17 to line 25 of our code. For our main function, we start off by getting an input from the user, and store than input inside the 'message' variable. You can clearly see this in line 18 of our code. Next, we created a background thread. This consists of an AsyncWrite thread, which in turn consists of '*message*' that is saved in *out.txt*. Next, we entered the syntax *background.start()*, which will start the run function in our AsyncWrite to start the background thread.

Now that the thread is running, we print a message to the user saying "The program can continue to run while it writes to another thread." This would show that our main program is still running while the thread is running in the background and storing the file. We then make a mathematical check to see if the program is still indeed running. We do this by adding 100 + 400.

Next, we put the syntax background.join(). This is the method of the Thread class which waits until the thread is finished before resuming. Our main program will sit on this background.join() method until the thread is finished. To show the thread is already finished, we're inserted the syntax *print "Waited until the thread was complete."*

If you're following along, make sure that you don't have any typing errors before saving and running the file. If you do, it is likely that the program will output an error instead of executing correctly. Once everything is entered correctly, save and run the file.

> $ Python asyncWrite.py

Once you enter that command, Python will immediately ask you to enter a string. Go ahead and any string that you like. For this example we're going to enter the string 'The quick yellow dog jumped over the fat cat." Once you enter that, you should have a result similar to the one below:

> *Enter a string: The quick yellow dog jumped over the fat cat*
>
> *The program can continue to run while it writes in another thread*
>
> *500*
>
> *Finished background file write to out.txt*

112

Waited until the thread was complete

Now, to verify if our program did indeed write the string that passed it into an out.txt file, go ahead and check your current directory if you have an out.txt file. To list every file in your current directory, type the syntax below and press ENTER:

$ ls

Once you enter that command, you'll have list of files in your current directory presented to you. Look for the out.txt file. If you have it, open it up in Vim using the syntax below:

$ Vim out.txt

Once you open the file, you should have the string that you entered at the beginning of the program written inside the file.

Locks

You may remember that the timer program that we created previously was printing out to the screen. Sometimes you can have issues where both threads will try to access the standard output, making the program print two different lines of output into a single line.

We can avoid this clashing of threads that use the same data by using Locks. Locks are pretty hard to understand at first. However, with frequent usage, you'll realize how easy it is to implement in code. We can use locks to lock access to one thread. Only one thread can be within a lock at a time.

To show how locks work, we'll go ahead and open the timer program that we previously created and modify it a little bit. What we'll do is put a lock around our timers, so that only one timer can use the print statement and output to the screen at a time.

Open your timer.py file and modify the code to match the one below:

```
1       import threading

2       import time

3

4       tLock = threading.Lock()

5       def timer(name, delay, repeat):

6               print "Timer: " + name + "Started"

7               tLock.acquire()

8               print name + " has acquired the lock"

9               while repeat > 0:

10                      time.sleep(delay)

11                      print name + ": " + str(time.ctime(time.time()))

12                      repeat -+ 1

13              print name + " is releasing the lock"

14              tLock.release()

15              print "Timer: " + name + " Completed"

16

17      def Main ():

18              t1 = threading.Thread(target=timer, args=("Timer1", 1, 5))

19              t2 = threading.Thread(target=timer, args=("Timer2", 2, 5))
```

```
20              t1.start()

21              t2.start()

22

23              print "Main Complete"

24

25     if__name__ == '__main__':

26              Main()
```

The first thing that we did is add a timer lock. We did this by typing the code at line 4. You'll also notice that our code in line 4 makes use of the whole threading library. So, at line 1, we're going to need to change *'from threading import Thread'* to *'import threading.'*

After we print that the timer has started in line 6, we're going to call *tLock.acquire ()* on line 7, and then print a message to the user at line 8. What the *tLock.acquire()* method will do is it will acquire a lock on the thread that called it first. We then let the user know that the lock has been acquire by a thread by printing the *'name'* and the string "*has acquired the lock.*"

Next, we need to make sure that it releases the lock. After our *'while'* statement, we will print out the *'name'*, plus the string, "*is releasing the lock.*" After it prints, we release the lock by typing the syntax *tLock.release()*. This is done so it can allow another thread to acquire it.

Lastly, we need to come down to our main and put 'threading.Thread' instead of just 'Thread' in both out T1 and T2 thread variables. We need to do this because we're now using the threading library, rather than a specific thread within that library. If you're following along, save and run the file. You should have an output like the one below:

Timer: Timer1 Started

Timer1 has acquired the lock

Main Complete

Timer: Timer2 Started

Timer1: Tue Aug 30 17:29:57 2016

Timer1: Tue Aug 30 17:29:58 2016

Timer1: Tue Aug 30 17:29:59 2016

Timer1: Tue Aug 30 17:30:00 2016

Timer1: Tue Aug 30 17:30:01 2016

Timer1 is releasing the lock

Timer: Timer1 Completed

Timer2 has acquired the lock

Timer2: Tue Aug 30 17:30:03 2016

Timer2: Tue Aug 30 17:30:05 2016

Timer2: Tue Aug 30 17:30:07 2016

Timer2: Tue Aug 30 17:30:09 2016

Timer2: Tue Aug 30 17:30:11 2016

Timer2 is releasing the lock

Timer: Timer2 Completed

As you can see, Timer1 has started, Timer1 has acquired the lock, and then says that the main function is complete. After that, we see that Timer2 has started. However, only Timer1 is allowed to print an output since it still has the lock. After Timer1 outputs five times, it then releases the lock and we get a notification saying that Timer1 has completed its task.

Since the lock has been release by Timer1, Timer2 now acquires it and then starts printing its output. After it prints its output five times, it release its acquisition of the lock and gives a notification that Timer2 has completed its task.

As you can see, locks are pretty easy to implement in code. Essentially, when one lock is acquired, nobody else can acquire that lock until it gets release by the function that called it first.

Semaphores

There's also a type of lock called Semaphores. Similar to locks, Semaphores restrict access to a thread. However, Semaphores allow more than one lock to be acquired. Let's say you have 10 threads trying to load up 10 different webpages, but you may only open up two or three connections at a time to stop the server from rejecting your request.

In this situation, what you can do is just set up a semaphore that restricts access to more than three threads, so that you can stay within the limited amount of connections that the server allows.

Chapter 16 Serialization in Python using Pickle

In this chapter, we'll be looking at using Pickle to dump objects to a file. So what is Pickle? Pickle is the standard package that comes with Python. It gives the functionality of 'Pickling' and 'Unpickling' objects in Python. Pickling is the process of converting a Python object hierarchy into a byte stream to be written to a file, or even a socket.

This is more commonly known as Serialization. However, to avoid confusion, the process is called pickling. Unpickling is the reverse process of turning a byte stream back into a Python object of the same state it was saved in. The standard library also comes with a *C* counterpart called '*C pickle*,' and can be up to a thousand times faster.

What Can It Do?

So what can Pickle do? Pickle is able to store and reproduce dictionaries and list, as well as lists that reference to other objects. Pickle can also store object attributes and restore them back to the state they are in before.

What Can't It Do?

So what can't Pickle do? It is important to realize that Pickle doesn't store any code from an object. It will only save the attribute's values. Pickle also cannot store attributes, their file handles, or their sockets. Also, it should be understood that C pickle cannot be used if you want to turn pickler, or unpickler, into a sub class.

Pickle Methods

Let's quickly have a look at the two methods that most Python programmers use for Pickling.

- **Dump** - The method dump will save the object it is given into a file stream you provide it. There is also an optional argument for the protocol. Most of the time, you can leave it empty. However, use '-1' if you want to use the highest protocol to save any objects or lists that have references to other objects or lists.

- **Load** - We also have the Load method, which loads the next object in the file stream and returns the object.

Pickling Program

Let's go ahead and create a Python program called 'pickling.py.' We'll use this just to simply see how pickle can dump and load dictionaries and lists. We'll create a dictionary and a list, and then dump them into a file. We'll then load them back into new objects and see if they're the same. Go over to your terminal and create a 'pickling.py' file using *Vim*.

$ Vim pickling.py

Once you're in the file, type the code below:

```
1       import pickle

2

3       dict1 = {'a': 100,

4                'b': 200,

5                'c': 300}

6

7       list1 = [400,

8                500,
```

```
9              600]

10

11      print dict1

12      print list1

13

14      output = open("save1.pkl", 'wb')

15

16      pickle.dump(dict1, output)

17      pickle.dump(list1, output)

18

19      output.close()

20

21      print "-----------"

22

23      inputFile = open("save1.pkl", 'rb')

24

25      dict2 = pickle.load(inputFile)

26      list2 = pickle.load(inputFile)

27      inputFile.close()

28

29      print dict2

30      print list2
```

So as you can see from our code, we imported the Pickle package in Python. We then defined our dictionary and list in lines 3

120

through 9 in our code. After defining them, we made use of the print command to print them out on the screen.

As you can see in line 14 of our code, we created our file stream. We made use of the variable 'output,' which would open a file named 'save1.pkl' in write binary 'wb' mode. Remember to use write binary or it won't work.

Next, we dump out our two objects--*dict1* and *list1*--in lines 16 and 17 of our code. As you can see, we did this by calling in pickle to dump both objects to our file stream, which is the variable 'output.' After dumping everything in the variable 'output,' we close our file stream using the 'output.close()' syntax. Lastly, we print a bunch of dashes to mark the separation of our two files.

Now, to load the files, we first created an 'inputFile' variable that opens up our previously saved 'save1.pkl' file. Note that this time this is in 'rb,' or read binary mode. Next, we create the two objects that we will load the data into. The first object is dict2, which is where we will load the dict1 file taken from the inputFile. The second object is list2, which is where we will load the list1 file taken the inputFile.

Once everything is loaded, we close the *inputFile* in line 27, and then print both objects--*dict2* and *list2*-- in lines 29 and 30 of our code.

After you type everything in, save and run it. After running it, you should have the output below:

> {'a': 100, 'c': 300, 'b': 200}
>
> [400, 500, 600]
>
> --------------
>
> {'a': 100, 'c': 300, 'b': 200}
>
> [400, 500, 600,]

Custom Class

We can also save objects of our own custom classes. We can then load saved objects of that class into any other program as long as Pickle can access that class file. Also, make sure that the class of that object is in the same directory as your program, or installed in the Python lib directory.

Player State Save

Now, let's go ahead and create a custom class called "Player." In that class, we'll store an ID, name, health, and list of items that the player has. We'll then save that object of the class Player using Pickle, and then load it back into a separate object. So let's call our player class file 'Player.py,' and we'll call our program 'savedata.py.'

First create our player class file by typing the syntax below:

```
$ Vim Player.py
```

Inside our player class file, type the code below:

```
1       class Player
2           def__init__(self, ID, name, health, items):
3               self.id = ID
4               self.name = name
5               self.health = health
6               self.items = items
7
8           def__str__(self):
9               return "My ID: " + str(self.id) + \
10                  "\nMy Name: " + self.name + \
```

| 11 | "\nMy   Health: "   + str(self.health) + \ |
| 12 | "\nMy Items: " + str(self.items) + "." |

Once you typed everything, save and close it. So you now have the Player.py class file. Now, we'll create our *savedata.py*.

$ Vim savedata.py

Once you have your savedata.py open, type the code below:

```
1     import pickle

2     from Player import Player

3     items = ["axe" , "sword" , "gun"]

4     myObj = Player(1, "JEFF", 100.00, itmes)

5     print myobj

6     with open("save2.pkl", 'wb') as outfile:

7                    pickle.dump(myObj, outfile)

8     print "--------------------"

9     newObj = None

10    with open("save2.pkl", 'rb') as infile:

11                   newObj = pickle.load(infile)

12    print newObj
```

Once you typed everything correctly, save and run the file. Running the file should give you the output below:

My ID: 1

My Name: JEFF

My Health: 100.0

My Items: ['axe', 'sword', 'gun'].

My ID: 1

My Name: JEFF

My Health: 100.00

My Items: ['axe', 'sword', 'gun']

As you can see, program has successfully take all the date from our customer class, which is Player.py, and then dumped it into a new object and then printed it out and displayed on the screen. Also, if you look in your current directory after running this program, you'll have two pickling files, specifically *save1.pkl* and *save2.pkl.*

If you open save2.pkl to see what's going on, you'll see the pickling file's basic protocol. As you'll see, there's an instance of 'Player,'--it will try to load in a player class if it can access it--the list of items, its health, its ID, and its name. If you open up save1.pkl, you'll see that it has the output1, which is 'a', 'b', 'c', and their corresponding values.

Here are some extra bits of information that are essential for you to know about Pickle:

- Pickle is cross-platform. What this means is you can save an object on Linux and then open it in Windows. However, pickle is known to have issues with different versions of Python. So as much as possible try to keep the same Python versions across platforms.

- If you use the dump function more than once on a file stream, you must use the load function just as many times to pull the data out.

- Finally, never trust pickle data from an untrusted source. Malicious objects can be unpickled using the standard library as a weapon against you.

Database Interaction

So what is database interaction? Interaction with the database is the connecting to, and querying of, a database. This could be inserting new data, creating new tables, deleting data, modifying data, or just viewing data. These databases can be on web servers, the local machine, or even database files.

We use SQL, or Search Query Language, to talk to databases. And we can use Python to send those commands. This is great for programs that need to store lots of data, scripts that manage or cleanup databases, scripts that backup the database, and many more.

Python sports a wide range of databases. Python has written a standard on how modules should communicate with a database. This means that all the different modules that talk to a certain database, all have the same methods. Some of the supported databases are things like MySQL, Microsoft SQL server, SQlite, ORACLE, and many more.

Methods for Database Interaction

Let's quickly have a look at the main methods we use for database interaction.

- **connect(info)** - First, we have the connect method. This is the first method we use when we want to talk to a database. The connect method is usually the only method that will have differences from other modules. Most of the time, this method will take an address, a user, and a password. However, there will be times when it will take an address, a user, a password, and a database name. Other times it would just take the database name.

- **cursor()** - Next, we have the cursor method. This method will return a new cursor object that allows the executing of queries and holds the temporary data.

- **execute()** - We then have the execute method, which belongs to the cursor object. It executes a single SQL statement.

- **fetchone()** - The fetchone method also belongs to the cursor, grabbing the first row of data that is in the current query result.

- **fetchall()** - The fetchall method is pretty similar to the fetchone method. However, it returns a list of litsts of the currect query result.

- **commit()** - The commit method belongs to the connection object. It saves any changes made to the database in the preceding queries.

- **rollback()** - The rollback method rolls back any temporary changes made in the preceding queries. This is pretty much the opposite of the commit method.

- **close()** - The close method also belongs to the connection object. Its main function is to just safely close the connection.

- **executemany()** and **executescript()** - Finally, we have the executemany and executescript methods. These methods execute multiple queries on the database. One is parameter based, and the other is a single script.

Conclusion

Congratulations for finishing this book, I hope it was able to equip you with the essential skills and fundamental knowledge to explore and harness the powerful features of Python as a programming language. By the time you finished reading the book, I am confident that you will be prepared to put your basic programming knowledge to practical everyday uses.

The next step is to take up advanced Python programming courses that will help you create more complex programs such as games, web applications, and productivity tools.

Finally, if you enjoyed this book, please take the time to share your thoughts and post a positive review on Amazon. It'd be greatly appreciated!

Thank you and good luck!

8238792R00078

Printed in Germany
by Amazon Distribution
GmbH, Leipzig